Miranda Threlfall-Holmes is Vicar of Belmont and Pittington in the Diocese of Durham, and an honorary fellow of Durham University. Previously, she was Chaplain and Solway Fellow of University College, Durham, and a member of the Church of England General Synod. She has first-class degrees in both history (from Cambridge) and theology (from Durham), and a PhD in medieval history. She trained for ordination at Cranmer Hall, Durham, and was then a curate at St Gabriel's church in Heaton, Newcastle upon Tyne. She has taught history at Durham and Newcastle universities, as well as for the North East Institute for Theological Education, the Lindisfarne Regional Training Partnership and Cranmer Hall. As a historian and theologian, she has written and published extensively in both the academic and popular media. Her doctoral thesis, *Monks and Markets: Durham Cathedral Priory 1460–1520*, was published by Oxford University Press in 2005, and she co-edited *Being a Chaplain* with Mark Newitt in 2011 (published by SPCK). She has also contributed to the *Church Times*, *The Guardian* and Reuters.

THE ESSENTIAL HISTORY OF CHRISTIANITY

MIRANDA THRELFALL-HOLMES

First published in Great Britain in 2012

Society for Promoting Christian Knowledge
36 Causton Street
London SW1P 4ST
www.spckpublishing.co.uk

British Library Cataloguing-in-Publication Data
A catalogue record for this book is available from the British Library

ISBN 978-0-281-06642-1
eBook ISBN 978-0-281-06643-8

Typeset by Caroline Waldron, Wirral, Cheshire
First printed in Great Britain by Ashford Colour Press
Subsequently digitally printed in Great Britain

Produced on paper from sustainable forests

Contents

v

Acknowledgements

This book has grown out of a lecture course that I devised and delivered to trainee Readers and Ordained Local Ministers in Newcastle Diocese for the North East Institute for Religious Education, in 2003–6. My thanks go first of all, therefore, to all those who took that course; I greatly enjoyed teaching you and learning with you, and this book is the better for your feedback and questions. Thanks also to the students of Cranmer Hall Theological College, and the Lindisfarne Regional Training Partnership, who (sometimes unwittingly) tested parts of this material in 2011–12. Among them I am particularly grateful to Andy Stinson and Mike Loach, who gave me detailed feedback on some new sections. I am grateful to Ruth McCurry of SPCK for commissioning this book, and for her professional advice and personal encouragement.

In writing this book I have necessarily drawn on a wide range of secondary literature as well as primary sources. The most useful of these are listed in the references and suggestions for further reading at the end of this book, but I am of course indebted to many more than those. I hope that I have acknowledged all quotations, but I am uneasily aware that, over several years of teaching this material, I may have inadvertently adopted someone else's phrasing as my own. I apologize in advance if that is so.

On a more personal level, I gratefully acknowledge my book group (Laura Mazzoli Smith, Anne Bennett, Mary McMahon, Angela Woods, Marita Grimwood, Rachel Volland and Corinne Holmes) who have given me the invaluable support and encouragement of fellow readers and writers, as well as help with childcare as the deadline approached. The members of the Ecclesiastical History Seminar of Durham University, especially my co-chair Alec Ryrie, have also been a supportive and reflective group, and a pleasure to know. Finally, I am especially grateful to my husband Phil, not simply for his tireless love and support but also for his time and care in reading and commenting on this entire book in draft form. This book is for him.

Introduction

The history of Christianity can seem a dauntingly large one. It covers 2,000 years – more, if its roots and Judaic prehistory are to be adequately accounted for. It covers virtually every corner of the world, and not simply sequentially but in a complex and overlapping sequence of movements, retreats and conflicts. And, as it has been received into different cultures and periods, it has been refracted – like a rainbow in a prism – into a dazzling spectrum of different shades. As a result, there is never a time at which we can point to one, monolithic grouping and say 'Look – there is Christianity as it originally was; now let's see what happened to it'. Right from the beginning, the movements inspired by Jesus were disparate in geography, outlook, cultural and religious background, social class and nationality.

Theological differences in emphasis and in substance were the inevitable result. This seems to have been a logical result of a religion which began, so its adherents believe, with the incarnation (literally, the 'en-fleshing') of God in one particular time and place. This is a religion whose main doctrine has never – contrary to much popular opinion – been contained between the covers of a book, but in the lived experience of a human, historical person. It follows logically and inevitably that there is no one 'correct' form of Christianity, but as many different relationships to that person as there are people in relationship with him.

Logical and inevitable this kaleidoscope of faith may be, but it remains dauntingly complex. Nevertheless, if we allow our focus to move away from the intricate historical detail, and instead zoom out to the big picture of the past 2,000 years of Christian history, clear story-arcs, themes, and contours of development can be seen.

This is important not just because it enables us to understand what has gone on in the past, but because the past has shaped the present reality. Understanding the big picture of Christian history therefore helps us to understand what has shaped our present experiences of churches, religion, spirituality and religious conflict. It also gives us important clues as to what might happen in the future.

The aim of this book is for you to gain an overall understanding of the broad sweep of Christian history. The book is not primarily concerned with facts and dates, but with trends, long-term developments, and the context of particular events. There will of course be some facts and some dates: these are examples, evidence that has helped historians to pick out the trend that is being illustrated. They will not be exhaustive, but I have tried hard to ensure that they are representative. That is, while this is necessarily a summary of a very big subject, the examples given have been chosen to be typical of the periods and developments being discussed. Please don't be afraid of the dates involved – you are not expected to learn them! If you want to refer to a particular fact or date again, it will be right here where you left it. Should you want more detailed information about a particular period or subject, you will find suggestions for further reading at the end of the book.

I hope that you enjoy this book, that you will be inspired and intrigued, and perhaps moved to pick up some of the suggestions for further reading. And I hope that you will be left, not with a mind full of dates, but with a sense of the shape of the landscape, understanding and appreciating the view, and with some clues as to what might be around the next corner.

Ways to use this book

Individuals

This book is a quick and easy read. It is short enough for the whole book to be read in one or two evenings, to give you a quick overview of the whole of Christian history. Or, if you only have small slivers of time available, the short chapters mean that it can be read in several brief bursts.

In writing this book, the main audience I've had in mind is Christians who want to deepen their knowledge and understanding of Christianity. You might be reading simply for your own pleasure, or you might be undertaking some formal further study, perhaps training for ordination or to be a reader, or taking an evening course. In that case, I hope that this book will provide an overview of the context into which more detailed study will fit. While some will read it as a whole, from start to finish, others will no doubt dip into a particular chapter to provide some context for an essay or other piece of study. The chapters have therefore been written so as to be largely self-contained, and cross-references given where necessary to relevant material that can be found in other chapters.

Groups

In testing early drafts of this book with members of local churches, several people suggested that they would value using the book for group study, either as a Lent course or as the basis for a series of cell group meetings. For many such groups, and particularly for Advent or Lent courses, a series of four or five meetings is the most common pattern. I have therefore suggested, on page xii, four 'pathways' of selected chapters, three of five weeks and one of four weeks, which can be used in this way. The bracketed chapter in each of the first three pathways can be omitted to provide a coherent four-week alternative. You might also, of course, choose to use the entire book, perhaps split into the two blocks suggested by Path 1 and Path 2; or make up your own selection based on the interests of the group.

Over several years of teaching church history to ordinands, clergy, readers and undergraduates, I have found that most people are nervous of the subject, as being too vast to do justice to, but also tend to know more about it than they give themselves credit for. Where they struggle is in relating the various facts that they know to one another, and putting them in their historical contexts. We often begin a new course with a long roll of paper, on which I write at one end '0' and at the other '2000'. I then invite the group to call out facts or incidents that they know of, and together we agree on whereabouts on the makeshift timeline they should be placed. People usually begin the evening feeling that they know nothing about Christian history and that it is too big a subject to be easily grasped, and end the first hour or so surveying the timeline – now crowded with writing – in disbelief that they knew so much.

You may like to try this exercise for yourselves, in your first group meeting. You can use old wallpaper or a children's art paper roll, or simply several sheets of A4 paper taped end to end. It might help to begin by writing the events or incidents that come to mind on sticky notes, so that you can reposition them easily. This can also represent any uncertainty as to where exactly things go; knowing that they can be easily moved can help to remove any 'performance anxiety' associated with this exercise. You might like to keep your timeline, and refer to it again when you've read the rest of this book.

Path 1: Early Christian history

Week 1: Chapter 1: Christian beginnings
Week 2: Chapter 2: The imperial Church
Week 3: Chapter 3: European conversion
Week 4: Chapter 4: Western Christendom
(*Week 5*: Chapter 5: Beyond Western Christendom)

Path 2: Modern Christian history

Week 1: Chapter 6: Reformation and Counter-Reformation
(*Week 2*: Chapter 7: The longest Reformation)
Week 3: Chapter 8: The modern period
Week 4: Chapter 9: Globalizing Christianity
Week 5: Chapter 10: Christianity after *c*. 1900

Path 3: The history of the Church in and of England

Week 1: Chapter 3: European conversion
Week 2: Chapter 4: Western Christendom
Week 3: Chapter 7: The longest Reformation
Week 4: Chapter 8: The modern period
(*Week 5*: Chapter 10: Christianity after *c*. 1900)

Path 4: Christian mission through history

Week 1: Chapter 1: Christian beginnings
Week 2: Chapter 3: European conversion
Week 3: Chapter 5: Beyond Western Christendom
Week 4: Chapter 9: Globalizing Christianity

1

Christian beginnings: to *c.* 300

Introduction

Christian history begins with the history of Jesus' public ministry and the immediate aftermath of his death. Although there is considerable debate between Christians and non-Christians as to who exactly Jesus was, and what he did, there is no substantial argument as to the historical fact that someone called Jesus lived and taught in the area around Galilee and Jerusalem during the period of the Roman occupation of Palestine. There is considerable evidence from Christian, Jewish and Roman sources that Jesus existed, taught, and was executed by crucifixion, and that this execution was quickly followed by claims that he had risen from the dead.

Accounts vary as to the exact length of time that Jesus' public ministry lasted, but it seems to have been between one and three years. It ended with his execution just outside the city walls of Jerusalem some time between AD 29 and 32, on the day now commemorated as Good Friday. According to the Bible and Christian tradition, he was resurrected from the dead three days later, on the day now commemorated as Easter Sunday, and was seen and encountered by many different groups of people over the following 40 days. After that period, Luke, the author of the Acts of the Apostles, tells us that Jesus ascended into heaven (Acts 1.6–11). The bereft disciples were then given the gift of the Holy Spirit, an event commemorated in the Christian calendar as the feast of Pentecost, and the history of the Church is commonly dated from that point onwards.

At the beginning of this period, however, it is anachronistic to speak of 'Christianity'; the term was not in widespread use at this point. The first Christians thought of themselves as the fulfilment of classical Judaism, with Jesus being understood as the long-promised Jewish Messiah. Outsiders, such as the Romans, seem to have understood them as a variant sect within Judaism, and initially it seems that Christianity was primarily preached and successful within the context of the synagogues (Jewish worshipping communities). Christianity rapidly spread throughout the Roman Empire and beyond, helped by the presence of a common language, good trading networks and transport routes, and the extensive presence of Romans who respected and were interested in Judaism.

Its early spread was patchy, with particular concentration in cities and with some regions more affected than others, and exact statistics for its spread are impossible to calculate. However, by the beginning of the fourth century (*c.* AD 300) around half the population in some areas were Christian, and there were few parts of the empire where Christianity was unknown. Throughout this period there were sporadic periods of persecution, particularly fierce in the period after AD 250 when the Roman Empire was beginning to find its borders threatened. However, these were never severe or consistent enough to wipe out Christianity, but instead gave it both publicity and a self-understanding of purity and separation which has proved remarkably persistent and influential in later centuries.

The beginning of Christianity

After the events of the first Easter, there was a small but highly committed core of people who believed both that Jesus was in some way God, and that he had risen from the dead. Since these were the earliest core beliefs, they have a plausible claim to be the heart of the Christian faith. Many of the doctrines and teachings that have subsequently been held to be essential – that Jesus died to save us from our sins, or the doctrine of the Trinity, for example – were not at this point precisely formulated, though it seems highly likely that they were held by at least some of the earliest Christians. Nor was the term 'Christian' in widespread use at this point. The earliest disciples were not yet clearly differentiated from mainstream Judaism. It was generally believed that Jesus had come to revive and restore Judaism, rather than found a new religion. It was only as conflicts with the traditional Jewish authorities increased that this changed. These conflicts escalated as Judaism was particularly concerned to define its boundaries after the destruction of Jerusalem by the Romans following successive Jewish revolts against Roman rule in AD 66–70 and 132–5. By the early to mid second century, therefore, the two had clearly diverged into two distinct religions.

The earliest known use of the word 'Christian' comes in the Acts of the Apostles, probably written around AD 60–70 (Acts 11.26). Both the fish (*icthys* in Greek, which also served as an acrostic for Jesus Christ, Son of God, Saviour) and the cross were well-known Christian signs, certainly from the second century onwards, being used in inscriptions and referred to in Christian writings. The crucifix (a representation of Christ crucified, rather than simply a bare cross) only developed as a Christian symbol after it had stopped being used as a routine Roman punishment, and is only known from the fifth century onwards. Earlier than this, however, it was used as a slur. One of the best-known pieces of early graffiti is a crude cartoon of a man with a donkey's head being crucified, which we know dates from before AD 79, as it was found in the excavations at Pompeii. It shows a man kneeling before the cross with the slogan 'Alexamenos worshipping his God' (Green, 2004).

Over the last few decades a great deal of light has been shed on the religious context in which Christianity developed, above all with the discovery of the library of the Qumran community (popularly known as the 'Dead Sea Scrolls'). These documents reveal that the Judaism of the century or so before Jesus lived was full of renewal movements, hermits, quasi-monastic communities emphasizing bodily holiness and denial, apocalyptic predictions, and so on. In this context, John the Baptist (Luke 3.1–18) would have been seen as simply one of a long line of eccentric prophets calling for repentence; those who went out to be baptized by him would have been acting in a culturally accepted way. Similarly, the initial preaching and teaching ministry of Jesus would have been of a type that was widely familiar.

This explains two otherwise puzzling and contradictory things about the Gospel accounts. On the one hand, we are told that thousands of people followed Jesus (think of the feeding miracles, and his having to teach from a boat); on the other, that it was not clear to more than a handful of close followers that he was anything very different, and even they remained unconvinced until after the resurrection. Contemporary documents illuminate very clearly that this was a period in which charismatic teachers and miracle workers were a common and accepted part of life. There was what we might almost call a celebrity culture around them, in which a gathering of hundreds or even thousands was not an unexpected occurrence, but a good day out. This explains the apparent paradox that few took Jesus particularly seriously at the time; he was one among many, and only after the resurrection did his uniqueness become clear.

The early spread of Christianity

Christianity began to spread remarkably quickly after the initial events of the first Easter and Pentecost, both within the local Jewish community in Jerusalem and much more widely. This was partly due to intentional missionary activity on the part of the earliest Christian leaders, but three structural factors were also critically important. These were the presence of a common language; the infrastructure of the Roman Empire; and the wide cultural and religious penetration of Judaism throughout the empire.

The earliest Church spoke Aramaic, the local language and Jesus' own mother tongue. But most early Christians would also have spoken and understood Greek, which was the lingua franca of the Roman world (not Latin, which was simply one local language among many). Indeed, Greek was widely understood even beyond the limits of the empire: the conquests of Alexander the Great in the fourth century BC had spread Greek well into Asia, and there was a Greek kingdom for two centuries in and around India. Greek was very widely spoken as a second language, and this meant that there was little or no language barrier in communicating the gospel message. The earliest texts of the New Testament were written in simple, idiomatic Greek, and would have been easily understood across disparate societies and social groups.

From the beginning, it is clear that the Church was multinational, as the Pentecost story graphically illustrates (Acts 2.1–11). This is not surprising, as the Roman world was extremely multicultural because of widespread trading networks, the institution of slavery, and the fact that soldiers were always posted to other countries than their own. The famous *Pax Romana* (the Roman peace), though sometimes patchy and fragile, was a reality. Within the empire, travel was relatively safe, with piracy and banditry harshly punished. Good roads and sea routes linked all parts of the empire. It is quite remarkable how the early Christians managed to get about the world – much more easily, in some cases, than the believers who were to follow them a few hundred years later.

4

Many of the individuals who were the first believers would therefore have been very mobile, and as they travelled around the empire – as slaves, merchants, soldiers or government officials – they would have spread their faith widely. This is backed up by external evidence showing the rapid geographical spread of Christianity across the region and beyond, often following prominent trading routes. One of the most famous examples is a letter that Pliny the Younger wrote to the Emperor Trajan asking his advice, in around AD 112. Pliny was governor in the remote and mainly rural region of Bithynia, in north-west Asia Minor, and he was dismayed by the rapid spread of Christianity to 'many of all ages and every rank, and also of both sexes . . . [and not in] the cities only, but the villages and country' (Stevenson and Frend, 1987).

But an even more decisive factor may well have been the successful spread of Judaism itself in previous centuries. Jews were to be found everywhere throughout the empire, with synagogues in all the main cities. Graeco-Roman culture was fascinated by ancient wisdom, and monotheism was growing in attraction by this period. The old gods were increasingly understood, at least by the intellectual and cultural elite, to be mythological, and monotheism was viewed as a purer and more intellectually satisfying alternative. Some converts became Jews through circumcision, but circumcision was not generally a culturally acceptable practice in Hellenistic (Greek-influenced) society, so most Gentile adherents to Judaism remained 'God-fearers'. Through attendance at the synagogues they were well versed in the Old Testament and its moral and theological ideas, and they seem to have been the earliest respondents to the gospel. It has been suggested that 'It was the presence of this prepared elite that differentiated the missions of the apostolic age from those of every subsequent time, and makes comparison almost impossible' (Neill, 1986).

Though Christianity spread rapidly throughout the Roman empire, its progress was uneven in different areas. The empire itself was primarily city based; government and economy were centred on cities, and transport links were focused on providing routes for trade and information between cities. The growth of the early Church mirrored this organizational pattern. Initially, missionaries travelled to the major cities – Paul's journeys, described in Acts, being the best-known example. Paul was by no means the only full-time missionary in this early period, but he may well have been the most systematic, and is the one of whom we have most evidence. His technique was very much based on the great cities of the empire, settling in a major city for a time, and using his assistants to radiate out to the smaller cities of the region.

Estimating numbers for the spread of Christianity in this period is very difficult, since historians have to extrapolate from small fragments of documents and archaeological evidence. In around 250, for example, a letter from Bishop Cornelius of Rome recorded that the Christian community there included '46 presbyters, 7 deacons, 7 sub-deacons, 42 acolytes, 52 exorcists, readers and door-keepers, over 1500 widows and persons in distress' (Stevenson and Frend, 1987). It has been calculated that this represents a total Christian population of around 30,000. While the total population of Rome at this time is uncertain, this clearly represented a significant fraction of the total.

Progress was perhaps most rapid in those parts of North Africa comprising present-day Tunisia and Algeria. Here, Christianity may well have arrived from two directions simultaneously, both across from Egypt and south from Rome. It is certainly the case that the first Latin-speaking churches of the world were to be found in North Africa, and this is probably also where the first Latin Scripture translations were made. There is evidence of very many bishops from this region, one for almost every town and village, implying the existence of many thriving Christian churches. The most famous and lastingly influential early Christian writer, Augustine of Hippo, was born to a Christian mother, Monica, and a pagan father, in Tastage in North Africa around 354.

At the northern extremes of the empire, there seem to have been at least some Christians in Britain by the early years of the third century. In 208 the Roman theologian Tertullian claimed in his treatise *Adversos Judaeos* that by about 200 Christianity was established in the remoter parts of the empire, including even 'places of the British not approached by the Romans' (Hylson-Smith, 1999). Christians may have fled to Britain from the persecutions in Gaul, in 177, and there were well-established trade routes to Britain which Christianity might have followed: from Gaul to eastern Britain, or along the Mediterranean Sea and around the Spanish coast to the far south-west of Britain. The first named British Christian is Alban, whose story of hiding a Christian priest, being converted, and giving himself up in the priest's stead is related in Bede's *Ecclesiastical History*. The story is thought to be broadly true, and likely to have occurred in 304, during the Diocletian persecutions. But there would only have been a sprinkling of Christians in Britain at this period, perhaps a few traders and soldiers. There is no evidence of any organized church in Britain until after Constantine's 313 Edict of Milan (see Chapter 2).

So by the end of the third century almost no part of the empire was untouched by Christianity. On the eve of the dramatic change in fortunes that was about to occur for the Church with the conversion of the Emperor Constantine in 312, it has been estimated that out of a total population of around 50 million, perhaps 10 per cent were Christian. These were unevenly distributed across the empire, however. In some places, such as parts of Asia Minor, as much as half of the population may have Christian, whereas other areas were relatively untouched, and Christians were disproportionately concentrated in the major towns and cities.

It is also notable that Christianity had spread beyond the bounds of the Roman Empire by this point. For example, there is known to have been a Syriac-language church in Edessa in northern Mesopotamia. Eusebius, writing in the fourth century, quoted a legend of King Abgar writing to Jesus; even assuming that to be apocryphal, it is clear that the Syrian church was ancient by Eusebius' time. It is also possible that there is some truth in the legend that the Apostle Thomas personally founded the church in India. The legend has it that when he refused to make the journey, God arranged for him to be sold as a slave to an Indian king whom he then converted. Certainly the journey described in the legend was a possible one, the king is a real one from the period, and the Indian church is one of the earliest known. A similar story in relation to the founding of the church in Ethiopia is almost certainly factual. Two young Christian men from Tyre, who were shipwrecked while travelling down the Red Sea, were taken as slaves to the King of Ethiopia. They were subsequently appointed to high office and became free to preach the gospel. Years later one of them, named Frumentius, travelled to Alexandria to ask the bishop, Athanasius, to send priests to Ethiopia, and was himself consecrated Bishop of Ethiopia, probably in 341.

The earliest converts seem to have been mainly relatively low-status members of society: slaves, women, petty traders and some soldiers. A Roman critic of Christianity, Celsus, wrote disparagingly (in his *Against the Christians* in the late second century) of Christians teaching 'wool-carders, cobblers, laundry-workers, and the most illiterate and bucolic yokels' (Stevenson and Frend, 1987). But there were also always some higher-status individuals, particularly intellectuals who found the spiritual and philosophical answers they were looking for in the Christian message. For example, Justin Martyr (*c.* 100–165) described how he looked in all schools of philosophy for true wisdom, then met a Christian teacher at Ephesus and was converted.

The rapid spread of Christianity is startling in the context of a society in which an enormous variety of different religions coexisted. Justin Martyr's explanation of his conversion demonstrates the extent to which Christianity answered a need: this was a society in which many were increasingly unconvinced by the multiplicity of religions, and in which monotheism was increasingly attractive as a philosophical ideal. As already noted, Judaism had attracted many over the past centuries, but full membership of Judaism was hard to attain. In addition, Christianity does seem to have attracted converts by the moral standards upheld by its members. Roman society was widely recognized to be immoral and cruel; slavery, torture and practices such as exposing unwanted infants to die were commonplace. Christians rapidly established a reputation for being loving and caring, and in particular were well known for looking after their poor, the special task of the deacons. The earliest official definition of Christianity may well have been as a burial club, in a society in which having a decent burial was an important concern.

The extent to which Christian behaviour may have inspired conversions is encapsulated in a criticism of exactly this, from the time of the last persecution faced by Roman Christianity. This was under the Emperor Julian 'the Apostate' (332–63), who wanted to reverse the establishment of Christianity as the official religion of the empire. When he found it harder than expected to reinstate and reinvigorate pagan religion, Julian blamed his slow progress on Christian philanthropy, their 'benevolence to strangers, their care for the graves of the dead, and the pretended holiness of their lives'. Writing to the high priest of Galatia, he commended outdoing them in such good deeds: 'it is disgraceful that, when no Jew ever has to beg, and the impious Galileans support not only their own poor but ours as well, all men see that our people lack aid from us' (Stevenson, 1966).

Persecutions

Many Christian writings claim that the calm and dignified behaviour of Christian martyrs during times of persecution led to mass conversions of those watching. Although this is probably an exaggeration, Christians were certainly notable for facing execution and imprisonment on account of their faith with unusual fortitude. This does seem to have impressed many into finding out more about the faith that could both be worth suffering for, and could produce such remarkable peace of mind.

For the first 300 years of its existence Christianity was sporadically persecuted for being both unpatriotic and anti-social. For the most part, the very early Christian movement was left alone. There is more evidence of tensions and persecution from within Judaism in the first century of Christianity than from the Romans, who at this point did not distinguish Christianity from other Jewish sects. One early and particularly brutal exception was the Emperor Nero, who reigned from AD 54 to 68; he appears to have delighted in cruelty, and is especially notorious for having apparently had Christians set alight as garden lighting. As this example shows, persecution was sometimes fierce, but until around 250 it was sporadic and local.

Roman society was essentially pluralistic, and tolerated most forms of religion so long as they did not threaten civic obedience. Jesus, of course, was not put to death (so far as the Romans were concerned) for religious reasons, but because it was feared that he would lead or be the cause of civic unrest. But pagan religion and society were very much intertwined, and so Christians' refusal to take part in pagan ceremonies meant that they largely had to withdraw or abstain from public life and civic office – one reason why the majority of converts were from the lower social strata of society. This withdrawal could easily be seen as threatening to the fabric of society. Outbreaks of persecution therefore depended largely on local circumstances and the inclination of local governors. For example, Pliny (in the correspondence with Trajan already quoted, from the early second century) asked for advice on how to treat Christians because they were becoming an economic threat, apparently disrupting trade by refusing to eat meat offered to idols: the emperor advised him not to go looking for them. This attitude seems to have been broadly typical of this early period, and meant that Christianity could spread and flourish, to the point where even the most serious persecutions were unable to uproot it entirely.

Over the years, as the Christian movement grew in numbers and influence as described in the previous section, it began to be seen more consistently as a threat. The risk was perceived as a political one because the Roman emperor was portrayed and worshipped as quasi-divine; Christians, who refused to worship the emperor, were accused of insubordination, disloyalty and treachery. However, the Jews had been respected in the empire for centuries for their firmly monotheistic stance, and it was only after Christianity had clearly diverged from Judaism that the majority of Roman persecutions began. But again, it should be emphasized that, although sometimes vicious while they lasted, these periods of persecution were sporadic: the Romans were not particularly interested in people's religion per se, but whether they were good citizens.

The major persecutions came in the mid third and early fourth centuries. At this point, not only had Christianity spread to perhaps 10 per cent of the population but also the Roman Empire was increasingly insecure around its borders and was beset with power struggles and infighting. Among the recriminations and political manoeuvrings there was a strong thread of nostalgia for the 'good old days' of Rome, identified with the old gods and practices. In 250, the Emperor Decius, ascribing Rome's wavering fortunes to a lack of worship of the old gods, demanded sacrifices from every household.

What was new about Decius' demand was the systematic way in which it was enforced. The edict was backed up with the introduction of a system of certificates to certify that the household had complied, and was clearly widely complied with, as several examples of such certificates have been found by archaeologists. Christians were persecuted when they refused to comply – though many went along with the imperial demands, either actually sacrificing or perhaps in some places managing to simply purchase a certificate.

Even more intensive was the persecution of Christianity under the Emperor Diocletian in 303–5. This time, the aim was deliberately and explicitly to wipe out Christianity, and so it began by focusing on clergy, and destroying churches and books. Although this was again implemented unevenly across the empire, it has become known as the 'Great Persecution', and just under half of all known Christian martyrdoms date from this period.

Theological developments

Although when we look back over the story of the early Church it is one of astonishingly rapid growth, at the time Christians were puzzled and pained by the existence of widespread antipathy and resistance to their message. The earliest disciples seem to have expected Jesus' imminent return; when this had begun to seem less likely, they also had to deal with the fact that Judaism in general, far from accepting that Jesus was the Messiah, was instead persecuting and marginalizing the early Christians. The literature of the New Testament bears witness to the process of rationalization and theological explanation that went on in the early Christian communities in the face of these realities.

Christians also, as we have seen, then had to deal with the fact of sporadic persecutions. This led to significant cognitive dissonance; the early Christians had somehow to reconcile the facts of their being a relatively small, persecuted group with their belief in the final and decisive victory of Jesus and in their own identity as God's chosen people. Over the first 300 years, Christians responded by developing an identity and self-understanding of the Church as an alien in the world: Christians are pilgrims or strangers, whose true homeland is elsewhere (in heaven). They came to see themselves as called to be, like Jesus himself, despised and rejected but ultimately triumphant. Being an outcast in society became seen as central to faith. It was understood as a fulfilment of both the Old Testament and Jesus' own prophecies about suffering. Persecution began to be seen not as an inconvenient fact which called the truth of the faith into question, but as confirmation that they were doing the right thing. Success in worldly terms sometimes even became demonized, redefined not just as a distraction from holiness (which was by no means a new idea but typical of much Greek philosophy), but as positively inimical to faith. This development caused some problems in the following centuries when Christianity became mainstream and allied with political power, as we shall see in the following chapters.

As well as the various Gospels and letters that have become known to us as the New Testament, these first centuries were also a fertile period for other Christian writings, by major theologians, philosophers and bishops. These writers are now known collectively as the 'Church Fathers', from which this early period (together with the next couple of centuries, to around 450) is often known as the 'patristic' period. There was a pressing need in these early centuries to define and explain Christianity, both to try to persuade those who mocked it of its truth (or at least of its coherence and intellectual credibility), and to argue with other Christians over what form, exactly, Christianity was to take. Many of these writings were written against what are now known as heresies, meaning variant, unorthodox forms or distortions of Christianity. It is important to remember that at the time it often remained unclear for several centuries which of these variants would win out as orthodoxy. After the conversion of Constantine, as we shall see in the next chapter, it became a pressing concern of the emperor, as well as the Church, to establish an official line on such doctrinal debates as the nature of Christ or of God's relationship with creation.

In the aftermath of the systematic persecutions of 250 onwards, the fact that some Christians had given in to the imperial demands led to new theological debates about the extent to which, and the mechanism by which, those who had complied could be reconciled to those who had suffered persecution. These debates led ultimately to the development of the systematic penitential theology and practice which was so typical of the medieval Church. They also reinforced developing ideas about ecclesiology, the apostolic succession and the unique authority of bishops, as the bishops had to justify their claim to be able to forgive. In particular, the role of bishops (especially those who had evaded persecution by some strategic travelling) was under threat from the unofficial moral authority being accorded to those who had suffered for their confession of faith. Martyrs were of course still important, but especially threatening to official church order were those who had been imprisoned but survived, as many apostates turned to them, rather than to the church authorities, for forgiveness. It is in this period, therefore, that details of a systematic and ordered church hierarchy were laid down. For example The *Apostolic Constitutions* (which was written in the late fourth century, but refers to earlier practice) attempted to formulate the distinctions between the three Holy Orders of deacons, presbyters and bishops.

Early Christian worship

The earliest known Christian churches were not purpose-built structures but were converted from existing houses. The earliest identifiable church so far found, for example, is a converted house in a Syrian city on the Euphrates, Dura Europos. The city was abandoned after a siege in the middle of the third century, and during the siege many parts of the city, including the church, were buried to create earth fortifications, thus preserving them well. The church is easily identifiable from wall paintings showing scenes from the New Testament. It has separate rooms for worship and for baptism, but oddly no obvious place for an altar. The oldest known purpose-built church dates from the late third or early fourth century, at the Red Sea port town of Aqaba. This shows many of the features that were soon to become standard in church architecture, including a central nave oriented east–west, with side aisles and a chancel (probably separated from the nave by a substantial screen), and an adjacent burial ground.

We know only a little about the worship of the earliest Christian churches. One early manuscript, the *Didache* (dating from around 100) gives us the oldest reliable information about early Christian practices in its central section (Stevenson and Frend, 1987). This includes immediately familiar instructions about baptism, which should be administered 'in the name of the Father, and of the Son, and of the Holy Spirit', and by immersion in running water if possible, but failing that by pouring whatever water is available three times on the head of the candidate. Fasting is recommended on Wednesdays and Fridays, and for the day or two before baptisms, and Christians are told not to pray with Jews but to say the Lord's Prayer three times daily instead. The Eucharist is described, with first the cup of wine and then the bread being blessed and distributed. Wording is given for the prayers of blessing, and these would be broadly familiar to modern worshippers since they have been incorporated in various modern versions of the eucharistic prayer. Notably, however, the wording given does not refer to the Last Supper. The rule that only the baptized should partake of the Eucharist is laid down. Provision is also made for a thanksgiving after a meal; it is not clear whether this refers to a separate ritual, or was a part of the Eucharist.

Conclusion

Christianity grew rapidly over the first 300 years of its existence. By the end of this period, around 10 per cent of the population of the Roman Empire were Christians, though these were unevenly distributed. Christianity was more common in cities than in the countryside, and in the south and east of the empire than the north and west. Christianity had also spread beyond the empire; the movement of merchants, soldiers and slaves meant that some parts of the population were extremely mobile in this period. Although Christianity had experienced some brutal persecutions, these had originally been too sporadic, and the more widespread and systematic persecutions had come too late, to prevent its spread. Persecutions may even have helped to spread Christianity, through admiration of the behaviour and strength of belief of those who suffered. They certainly had an important impact on Christianity's self-understanding as standing apart from society, and this could be problematic in the coming centuries, when Christianity became mainstream.

Questions to ponder

- What are the main similarities and differences that you notice between the early Christians' context and our modern context?
- What aspects of the early growth and spread of Christianity might we be able to learn from today?
- Which aspects of modern culture clash with your understanding of Christianity? Can you identify any ways in which your understanding of God or the Church has been adapted to help you make sense of these?

2

The imperial Church: *c.* 300–450

Introduction

Perhaps the most dramatic and abrupt development in the history of Christianity came in 312–13, when the Roman emperor Constantine publicly converted. Despite a few setbacks along the way, this period saw the transformation of Christianity from a sporadically persecuted minority religion to the official religion of the empire. There then came the great period of doctrinal definition, as the emperor threw his authority behind efforts to define the limits of acceptable doctrinal variation in the interests of social and political unity. Theologians also grappled creatively with many questions of how and to what extent Graeco-Roman culture could be synthesized with Christian beliefs. Physical church buildings, liturgy and church organization flourished. Two other major developments which went alongside these proved more problematic for later centuries: a strong theology of the close relationship between church and state, and increasing interest in asceticism as a Christian ideal.

Another major change that occurred over this period was the shift in the centre of gravity of Christianity, from the Western to the Eastern parts of the empire, as Constantine moved his court from Rome to Constantinople. This shift was particularly marked after Rome fell to the Goths between 410 and 476. After that, it would be several centuries before Rome regained its earlier dominance in European Christianity.

The conversion of Constantine

On his father's death in 306, Constantine (247–337) was proclaimed Caesar at York in England by the Roman legions there. However, he was not the only claimant to the imperial throne, and so he spent much of the next few years fighting to establish his position. The legend has it that in 312, before the battle of Milvian Bridge, near Rome (in which he defeated his rival Maxentius), Constantine saw a cross above the sun in the sky, and heard the words 'Conquer by this [sign]'. He duly put the Christian Chi-Rho symbol on his banners, and went on to win the battle. A year later, in the Edict of Milan, he gave substantial new freedoms and recognition to the Christian churches. It is often claimed that at this point he made Christianity the official religion of the state, but in fact the Edict of Milan produced a situation more akin to official neutrality towards different religions. The Edict of Thessalonica in 380 came closer to declaring a Christian state, but nevertheless it has been estimated that half of all high-ranking Roman officials as late as the 390s were devotees of religions other than Christianity, mainly worshipping the traditional 'pagan' Roman gods.

It can plausibly be suggested that Constantine's conversion may have been more of a political move, trying to associate himself with a powerful God, than a genuine personal transformation in the sense that we would now understand the term 'conversion'. His new religion certainly did not prevent Constantine from having several of his family members murdered over the next few years, including his wife and his eldest son. Nor was he baptized until several years later, on his deathbed. But this last fact was not unusual. It was commonly believed at that time that baptism washed you from sins committed up to that point, but that you were meant thereafter to live blamelessly and could not be forgiven sins committed after baptism (on the basis of texts such as Hebrews 6.4–6). The disciplines and theologies of penance and absolution which became such a feature of the medieval Church were still in their infancy at this point, and, as emperor, Constantine would have known that he would still fight, condemn people to death, and no doubt be involved in other political manoeuvrings of doubtful morality. Delaying baptism to one's deathbed, to be on the safe side, was by no means an unheard-of tactic in this period.

Whatever the true state of Constantine's own faith, the effects on the Church were dramatic and immediate. With the 313 Edict of Milan, Christians throughout the empire were given freedom of worship. Property and goods confiscated in the Diocletian persecution ten years before were to be restored. From 315 the first Christian symbols are found on Roman coinage, and no pagan symbols appear on coins minted under Constantine after 323. The judgements and jurisdiction of ecclesiastical courts were officially recognized, and churches were permitted to receive legacies. In 321, Sunday was legally recognized as a day of rest in towns.

The fact that churches could now own property, and be left property in wills, combined with the new legitimacy given to Christianity, led to an explosion in church building. There are over 20 surviving churches in Rome whose foundations can be dated to the early fourth century, six of which were built on Constantine's orders, and many others in cities such as Milan and further afield. The oldest parts of the cathedral of Trier in Germany have been dated to 340, and the church of St George in Sofia, Bulgaria, was built at a similar date. Many more followed over the ensuing decades. Christianity suddenly became first respectable, then fashionable, and soon a professional and social advantage, which led to a flood of new converts. It has been estimated that the number of Christians in the empire at least quadrupled in the following century. By around 400, for example, it has been estimated that Christians accounted for around half of the population of the major city of Antioch; that is, about 250,000 people out of a population of at least half a million.

This success was unevenly spread across the empire, however. At the rural edges of the empire Christianity remained a minority religion far from the centres of either religious or secular power. There is considerable academic debate, for example, about how healthy English Christianity was when the Romans finally departed in the years around 410. It seems likely that Christianity had gradually penetrated English society over the preceding century, so that by the end of the Roman occupation it was well established but patchy, with some areas, such as the south-west and the far north, barely touched. Although church buildings are hard to identify from this early period, the Chi-Rho sign has been found in late Roman villa mosaics, the best example being that at Lullingstone in Kent, dating from around 345. Certain hoards of metalwork and artefacts with Christian connections have also been found from this early period, most notably the Water Newton hoard from Cambridgeshire. This was probably the communal property of a Christian group, and includes objects bearing a gilt Constantinian form of the Chi-Rho, as well as an inscribed cup which refers to the existence of a sanctuary or church. There were certainly at least some bishops in place by 314, as it is known that three English bishops attended the Council of

Arles in that year; and Athanasius described some unnamed English bishops as being among those who took his (orthodox) side at the Council of Nicaea in 325.

So Christianity spread quickly but unevenly in this new situation. But although the Church now had peace to grow, there were obvious dangers. Issues of superficiality of conversion, of corruption, power and questionable motivations rapidly became pressing. Not only could the Church now receive money, but bishops, as acknowledged community leaders, rapidly came to be appointed to public positions such as judges. Bishops therefore quickly became powerful in the secular world, and bishoprics and some other church positions became very valuable appointments. The impact of this sudden and dramatic change not just on church life and organization, but on the theology and teaching of the Church, is fascinating and instructive.

Church, state, and doctrinal definition

At first, the Church was understandably enthusiastic about the new situation. The most well known and best preserved evidence for this is the writing of Eusebius, a Roman historian who lived from around 263 to 339, and who in 314 was made Bishop of Caesarea. Having lived through persecution himself he hailed Constantine as the new Logos incarnate, almost a second Christ. He was the great deliverer of the Church, sent by God to bring people to him. All parties in the various doctrinal disputes that were raging seem to have found it natural to turn to the emperor, as the head of the Church, to solve their conflicts, presumably all hoping that he would come down on their side. The emperor, for his part, wanted nothing less than a divided Church: doctrinal disputes were proving extremely divisive, and it was clearly important for political unity that the Church could speak with one official voice. The first major church council, known as the First Ecumenical Council because of the wide (though by no means universal) participation of church leaders from around the empire, was therefore called, and met at Nicaea in 325.

The disputes that this council met to resolve had been going on for some considerable time. Particularly important were issues about the identity and nature of Jesus. These were raised in especially sharp form by Arius, a Libyan who lived from around 250 to around 336 and who argued, among other things, that Jesus was the first created being rather than himself being God. Other debates clustered around issues of the nature of creation, with some taking the line from Plato's classical philosophy that matter was inherently inferior to spirit. This was important to Christian theology because the argument then went on to say, first, that the Jewish creator god could not be the real God (because God wouldn't create matter), and, second, that Jesus – if he were really God – could not possibly have been really incarnate as a human being.

Because the emperor wanted unity, he appears to have listened to the debates and then sided with the views that seemed to command the most widespread support among the delegates. The council approved a statement of belief, the Nicene Creed, which is still used regularly in Christian worship today in its later (381) version. In the lines of the Nicene Creed, with its emphasis on Jesus' coexistence with God the Father, on the fact that God created all things, and on Jesus' bodily incarnation, it is still possible to trace the alternative views that were being rejected. The original version of 325 included a final clause making the rejection of some of these absolutely explicit:

> And those who say: 'There was [a time] when he was not,' and 'Before his generation he was not,' and 'He came to be from nothing,' or those who pretend that the Son of God is 'Of other hypostasis or substance,' or 'created,' or 'alterable,' or 'mutable,' the Catholic and Apostolic Church anathematizes.
>
> (Stevenson and Frend, 1987)

As well as settling the specific points at hand, therefore, the council also established the very concept of 'orthodoxy', that is, of there being one official interpretation of Christian belief from which no significant deviations would be tolerated.

The initial assumption was that the official orthodoxy, established at the major councils, would inevitably be the view that the imperial establishment would support. But this assumption soon began to be challenged, when Constantine's sons began to side with the Arians because of their popular support in some places. It thus became less clear that the emperor should unthinkingly be identified as Christ's right-hand man, and increasingly powerful bishops began to assert their independence. A new theory of separate religious and secular jurisdictions began to be proposed, notably by Ambrose, Bishop of Milan in the late fourth century, when Milan was the seat of the imperial court. Ambrose's appointment as bishop by popular acclamation was a surprise: he had to be hastily both baptized and ordained in order to be consecrated as bishop. Milan was a hotbed of controversy between Arianism and orthodoxy, and at one point Ambrose was commanded by Justinia, the mother of the under-age emperor, to hand over a church for the Arians' use. Ambrose refused, claiming that 'palaces belong to the emperor, the churches to the bishop' (Stevenson, 1966). The strong position that bishops were in by even this relatively early date was shown even more clearly in 390, when Ambrose excommunicated the Emperor Theodosius for several months as penance for the massacre of around 7,000 people at Thessalonica.

Debate about the relative spheres of influence that properly belonged to the Church and to the state continued. Augustine of Hippo's book *The City of God*, which reflected on the fall of Rome in 410, was particularly influential in suggesting that Christians should be concerned with the heavenly 'City of God' rather than earthly politics. Alongside these theological discussions there were practical developments that had a similar impact. Quite soon after Constantine's conversion, for example, it became common for bishops to be appointed as magistrates, and they became responsible for often valuable portfolios of church property. This led to the development of canon law, and the concept of ecclesiastical courts.

Nevertheless, it remained an axiom of orthodox belief that even bad emperors were appointed by God to rule, and that the civil authorities should be obeyed insofar as related to their sphere of influence, the civil state. As will be seen several times over the course of this history, however, ongoing debates about the appropriate relationship between church and state have provided a near-constant background noise to the history of Christianity over the past 2,000 years.

The Council of Nicaea was the first of a series of seven major Ecumenical Councils over the following centuries, which define this as a period of vigorous doctrinal exploration, debate and definition. The first two, Nicaea in 325 and Constantinople in 381, focused on the Trinitarian issues discussed above. For the next 300 years, the emphasis shifted slightly to the details of Jesus' personhood. The key question was what forms of words could best capture and guarantee that both the divinity and the humanity of Jesus were upheld, neither being confused nor separated. This issue was discussed at the third council in Ephesus in 431, which is famous for giving Mary the title *theotokos*, mother (or bearer) of God, to emphasize Jesus' literal birth as a human being. The fourth council, at Chalcedon in 451, stated that the two natures of Jesus were not destroyed or subsumed in being united – in other words, being God didn't swallow up the fact that Jesus was also a man, and vice versa. The fifth and sixth councils, at Constantinople in 553 and 681, both re-discussed and eventually reconfirmed the definition made at the Council of Chalcedon. The Seventh Ecumenical Council, held once again at Nicaea in 787, had a rather different agenda; we will come back to this in the section on the shift to the East of the empire.

This was also the period in which the official canon of Scripture was established. Biblical scholarship is very uncertain for the period before the fourth century, but it is thought that Constantine's commissioning of 50 Bibles for the church at Constantinople in 331 might have begun the process of formulating a canon. In 383, the Bishop of Rome, Damasus I (who was incidentally also the first Bishop of Rome to be referred to as 'pope' in his own lifetime), commissioned the first official Latin Bible. This text, which would be known as the Vulgate, was prepared over the following decades, and the list of books that Damasus gave to be included formed a firm basis for discussions of the canon. Augustine of Hippo then convened three councils to discuss the canon, from 393 to 419, all of which declared that only the books officially decreed to form the Old and New Testaments should be read in church. The canon as set then remains familiar today, though the exact status of some books (the Epistle to the Hebrews, James, 2 John, 3 John, 2 Peter, Jude and Revelation) remained the subject of debate for some years. The books known as the Apocrypha in Protestant churches after the Reformation were included within the Old Testament section at this date, though some were given prologues noting that their canonical status was unclear.

Christianity and Graeco-Roman culture

As we saw in Chapter 1, Roman society was inherently based on paganism. Temple worship and sacrifices to the classical gods were interwoven with the fabric of society, so that civic office, army service and social life were very hard to disentangle from pagan practices. As a result, many early Christians rejected participation in civil society as incompatible with Christianity. However, as Christianity grew and spread, and particularly once it became the religion of the emperor and higher-status citizens converted in increasing numbers, Roman society grew gradually more secularized.

The question of how Christians should relate to the prevailing culture thus became at once simpler (in practice) and more complex (in theory). For example, entering the army had been generally frowned upon for Christians (though as we've already noted, some of the earliest converts were soldiers, and generally remained in the army serving their contracted terms). After Constantine's conversion, however, the army could be conceived as fighting for the spread or protection of Christianity, and so the question was revisited. A theological distinction was drawn between just and unjust wars, and it began to be more common for Christians to enter the army, and even serve as high-ranking officers.

Considerable intellectual effort was expended by theologians and philosophers over this period in trying to define which elements of Graeco-Roman culture could or should be assimilated, rejected, reinterpreted or simply accepted as the status quo. When it came to the old Roman gods, the consensus was clear – these were to be entirely rejected. Any similarities between the old myths and the Bible were assumed to have been placed there by demons to mislead the faithful. There was considerable overlap, however, between paganism and classical literary culture, and here the view was more ambivalent. Christian education continued to be based on the classical literary canon, and both Augustine of Hippo and Basil of Caesarea recommended the study of pagan classics to the extent that they were useful.

Classical philosophy, similarly, was too widely respected and culturally embedded to be rejected out of hand. Although some, such as Tertullian, did consider it too to be the misleading work of demons, most of the Church Fathers saw themselves as philosophers. There was considerable pagan intellectual criticism of Christianity in these first few centuries: it was derided for being dependent on faith not reason, and the literary style of the Scriptures was lambasted by the literary elite. Even St Jerome, famous as a translator of the biblical texts, described the style of the prophets as 'repellent and rude'. In response, the Church Fathers described Christianity as the true philosophy to which previous attempts pointed. As we've already seen, Justin Martyr famously traced his conversion as a journey of discovery through the Stoics, Platonists and Neoplatonists, until he finally found the ideal philosophy of Christianity. Clement of Alexandria argued that God had given philosophy to the Greeks in the same way as he had given the law to the Jews, to prepare them for Christianity.

Furthermore, classical philosophy was widely understood as sharing with Christianity the desire for the truth, and it was considered that philosophies could be measured against the yardstick of how close they were to Christianity. So, for example, Plato was widely praised for being right that there is only one God, but he was seen as being wrong in his view that matter pre-existed any act of divine creation. Stoicism, meanwhile, was right that humanity could attain the truth through reason, but wrong in asserting that it was possible for us to attain perfection through our own efforts.

Finally, some aspects of pagan philosophy were even incorporated into orthodox Christian thinking. Notable examples are Plato's conception of God's being eternal and unchangeable, and the idea of dualism, that there is a fundamental distinction between body and soul. Neither of these are features of the Judaic tradition or derive from the biblical texts. But both were widely accepted concepts, and they became very influential in Christian theology. This fusion of Neoplatonism with early Christianity is especially associated with the writings of Augustine of Hippo, who was converted by Neoplatonist ideas. Augustine became the most prolific and influential of the Church Fathers, especially through his major works *The City of God* and the autobiographical *Confessions*.

Asceticism

The other approach to the question of how Christians should relate to the world was very different, but equally influential. This was asceticism, the practice of separation from the world in pursuit of holiness, usually involving some degree of physical self-denial. Asceticism took a wide variety of forms, from the familiar (sexual abstinence, fasting) to the extreme (such as one group that was not simply vegetarian, but would only eat watery vegetables such as cucumbers). The range of practices reflected a range of theological understandings. Some simply felt that bodily denial would assist them in prayer. At the other end of the spectrum, some felt that ultimately the Church was unnecessary to salvation, and that personal holiness was what conferred authority and salvation on individuals.

Asceticism was not a new idea: Christian asceticism developed in the context of a variety of similar cultural practices. For example, some pagan philosophies emphasized ascetic ideals, notably the Stoic and Pythagorean schools. Jewish culture also contained ascetic, quasi-monastic communities, such as that at Qumran, or the Therapeutai in Egypt. Much more widespread in Judaism, of course, was the basic concept of adhering to the law. Groups such as the Pharisees attached considerable weight to strict adherence to the law in order to attain righteousness. The developing canon of the New Testament writings, including much of the biographical detail of Jesus' and Paul's lives, also supported mild asceticism (though Jesus' was a subversive example, with his occasional attendance at drunken dinner parties requiring some interpretation).

The earliest form of Christian asceticism was probably family settings that eschewed social norms, possibly from the first century onwards. Although little evidence for this early period exists, there was some legislation banning the practice of a couple living together in deliberately celibate 'marriage'. Small monastic communities also appear to have developed relatively early. The letters of Basil of Caesarea (in the mid fourth century) refer to orders of virgins, and regulations show monastic norms such as the taking of vows emerging in this period.

The most famous example was the phenomenon of desert monasticism, which developed in Egypt in the third century. Antony, the best known of these 'Desert Fathers', moved to the desert to live as a hermit when he was about 20, in 270–1; by the time of his death in 356 (at the age of over 100), tens of thousands of others had followed his example. Some competed to be prominently isolated, such as Simon Stylites, renowned for living atop a stone pillar, dispensing advice and wisdom to those who flocked to see him. Others had a more communal existence as 'hermits' in an increasingly crowded desert: the community at Oxyrynchus eventually consisted of around 20,000 members. Although the Desert Fathers were also influential in the Western church through their writings and biographies (the early fourth-century *Life of Saint Antony* was the popular and definitive guide to asceticism), Western monasticism tended to be mainly urban, dominated by clergy, and typically communal rather than solitary.

Several factors contributed to the prominence of asceticism in Christianity in the imperial period. In the first place, it was an attempt to impose stricter boundaries on Christianity, in reaction against the new situation that Christianity suddenly found itself in after the conversion of Constantine. In the face of a flood of new converts, whose genuine conversion was felt to be questionable, an increasingly ascetic definition of what it meant to be a Christian began to develop. Rules on moral matters such as divorce, intermarriage with pagans, and so on all got stricter over the course of the fourth century. Second, asceticism developed as a means of maintaining the martyr spirit and sense of identity as a heroic minority that the Church had developed under the sporadic persecutions of the previous centuries. Martyrdom was no longer available as a means of demonstrating one's faith, so self-denial became an alternative means of finding (or identifying oneself as) a spiritual hero. Third, the ascetic life appears to have been a particularly attractive option for women, allowing them both a certain independence, and real influence.

From Rome to Constantinople

In order to ease administration and military organization, the Roman Empire had been divided into two, the Eastern and Western territories, by the Emperor Diocletian in AD 285. The division went along fairly intuitive lines of geography, culture and economy. The empire was reunified in the fourth century under Constantine, but after the death of the Emperor Theodosius in 395 it was permanently divided. Although Constantine ruled over the whole empire, he established his capital not in Rome but in his new city, Constantinople, which he dedicated as the 'new Rome' in 330. Constantinople, with its magnificent new Church of the Holy Wisdom (Hagia Sophia), was to be the centre of his newly Christian empire. Rome (and the Bishop of Rome) retained a certain amount of historical and religious prestige, however, not least because it was the place of St Peter's and St Paul's martyrdoms. The Council of Nicaea in 325 had recognized Rome's seniority, followed by the Sees (bishoprics) of Alexandria and Antioch. Over the fourth century, this pattern developed into a set of five major sees, Rome, Constantinople, Alexandria, Antioch and Jerusalem, and this was formalized at the Council of Chalcedon in 451.

However, a major change took place over the fifth century, as the Roman or Western part of the empire came to an end. In 410, the Goths, led by Alaric, sacked Rome. Although pagan critics of

Christianity blamed this disaster on the way in which the old Roman gods had been neglected, Alaric was in fact an Arian Christian and left the churches, and those who had sought shelter in them, alone. This was the beginning of the end for the Roman Empire. In 452, Attila the Hun invaded Italy. The Bishop of Rome went to meet him at Mantua, and persuaded him to turn his army back (though it seems likely that strategic considerations and supply lines were at least as influential in Attila's retreat). But in 455, the bishop could only persuade Genseric, leader of a Vandal horde, not to destroy Rome or its people in return for opening the city gates to him. The last official Roman Emperor of the West, Romulus Augustulus, was deposed by a Germanic warrior who became the first barbarian King of Rome in 476, and by 480 the Western Empire had come to an end.

But well before this, from 410, Constantinople had self-consciously assumed the mantle of civilization from Rome. Although Rome continued to be recognized as having a certain seniority, the concept of the Bishop of Rome being the 'pope', with ultimate authority, is a much later development. The term was first used in the late fourth century, and Gregory I, Bishop of Rome from 590 to 604, was an important figure in arguing for this new concept of papal primacy, but in reality such primacy was established only in the eleventh and twelfth centuries (see Chapter 4). Until the 750s, the Byzantine emperor had the right to confirm the election of each new Bishop of Rome.

Conclusion

In this period, then, the sudden conversion of Constantine radically changed the context in which Christianity existed, and shaped the ways in which it developed over the following century. Because Christianity suddenly became first legal, and then positively encouraged, the Church as we know it was able to develop, with both a built and an organizational infrastructure. The Church was also able to grow rich, and new ethical questions were posed in this period as a result. This new situation led to an ascetic reaction, which flourished alongside the burgeoning ecclesiastical structures. The imperial desire for unity led to the new concept of orthodoxy being established, and the official creeds and doctrines of the Church ever since were formulated in this period. The Church became very closely associated with the empire, and as the empire was divided between

East and West the Church developed increasingly independently in each, leading ultimately to the division between the Roman Catholic and Greek Orthodox denominations in subsequent centuries.

Questions to ponder

- What were the main effects on Christianity of Constantine's conversion?
- What impact do you think being an established church has today?
- How do you feel about the idea of 'orthodoxy' (right belief) in Christianity?
- What impact has the development of asceticism had on later Christians?

3

European conversion: *c.* 450–1000

Introduction

Christianity faced two major challenges between AD 500 and 1000. In western and northern Europe, following the end of the Western Roman Empire by 480, the various 'barbarian' tribes and kingdoms that filled the power vacuum were both an evangelistic opportunity and a potential threat to stability. Europe was fragmented into a complicated patchwork of tribes and kingdoms. Over the next 500 years, Christianity spread, unevenly at times, to the northern and western corners of Europe. By around the year 1000, virtually the whole population of western Europe was formally Christian. They had been baptized in infancy, and had never known or experienced earlier forms of pagan worship.

The situation was very different in the south and east. Here, the rapid rise of Islam in the seventh century led to constant pressure on those borders, and a contraction of Christian territories. Islamic forces spread rapidly outwards from 622 onwards, taking Palestine and Syria by 640, and Alexandria in 642. By 715 most of Spain was under Muslim control, and in 846 a raiding party plundered Rome itself. In 902 Sicily became Muslim, and the Islamic forces exerted constant pressure on the eastern parts of the old Roman Empire. This continued well beyond the period focused on in this chapter, culminating in the Islamic conquest of Constantinople in 1453. The expansion of Islam over this period effectively gave Christianity a southern and eastern border. Christianity became increasingly defined as a European and 'western' religion: the opposite of what might have seemed likely in 500. The churches of the eastern and western parts of the old Roman Empire also gradually diverged over this period, so that by 1000 it is correct to talk in terms of two Churches: the Roman (Catholic) and the Greek (Orthodox).

Early missionary methods

Encounters with Islamic cultures showed them to be highly developed and civilized. They evoked intellectual respect as well as military competitiveness, and were perceived as a major threat (see Chapter 5). In contrast, the barbarian tribes of the north presented a very different challenge. These northern cultures were often illiterate, and while the Church had experience in countering paganism under Rome, these tribes had no similar traditions of philosophical enquiry on which to base apologetic discussions. It was therefore generally believed that the process of conversion was two-fold, encompassing the civilizing of society as well as the making of disciples.

The major accomplishments of this period were repeatedly due to the same three factors that we've already seen to have been important in the early spread of Christianity within the Roman Empire: royal favour, the impact of martyrdom, and monasticism. The most common method used in this period was to first concentrate on making a society nominally Christian, and then to work on the long process of the conversion of hearts and lives. Most often and most simply, missionaries would concentrate on converting the local chieftains or king, and would then implement mass baptisms of their people. When a group became Christian in this way they were baptized without long delay (but usually at Easter or Pentecost). The long-term work of conversion of lives began after that. It was in this period that penitential discipline developed most fully, to allow for the fact that there would be many backslidings and failures along the way.

In this next stage of the task, monasticism was a key feature of the successful missionary endeavours. Pioneering monasteries were founded in newly converted regions to provide instruction and examples of Christian living, and locals were often recruited into these monasteries also. The fact that these monasteries were almost all in remote and rural areas meant that, simply to survive, the monks had to cultivate the land and carry out all the other subsistence tasks of the peasantry, as well as continuing the *opus dei* (the work of God) of their daily rounds of prayer. The fact that the monks lived and worked as local farmers tended to bring them into very close contact with the local population. As a result, they were often able to transform local beliefs and ceremonies by bringing sacred places and seasons into relationship with the liturgy and the Christian year.

These northern monks also celebrated and used the local vernacular cultures. The Latin cultures of southern Europe tended to think of the barbarian languages as irredeemably uncouth, but in the north these languages and the oral culture that they carried were valued. Latin remained the language of the liturgy but, from the earliest days of the northern missions, it is clear that the local languages that were encountered were considered to be worth preserving and using in the service of God, in songs, stories and teaching.

Ireland and Scotland: Monastic mission

Christianity flourished from surprisingly early in the most northerly and westerly parts of Britain. What is known about this 'Celtic' Christian growth is mainly based on the lives of the various saints who were the pioneering missionaries and evangelists of the period, and whose influence lived on for many centuries. Their various stories illustrate the variety and independence of Christian missionaries in this period. For example, St Ninian appears to have sailed to the north-west coast of Britain as a solitary missionary in around 397, having studied monasticism under St Martin at Marmortier in France. He quickly founded the monastery at Whithorn (in southwest Scotland), which then served as a base from which he and his monks set out on evangelistic journeys. These took them round Wales, up the east coast of Scotland and across the sea to Ireland. The monastery at Whithorn continued to be an important centre for some time, producing numerous other early saints such as St Kentigern (in the early sixth century).

A near contemporary of Ninian's was St Patrick, now famous as the patron saint of Ireland. Patrick's biography demonstrates well the instability of these early societies. He was born around 385 somewhere on the west coast of England, the son of a Roman civil official, and apparently the grandson of a Christian priest. At the age of 16 he was captured in a raiding party and taken to Ireland as a slave, where he lived for the next six years, herding cattle and apparently receiving some basic education. It is not known where exactly he was for the next 15 years, but he must have received training for the priesthood. It seems possible that at some point he escaped to Gaul, and like Ninian had some contact there with St Martin. Eventually Patrick was able to return home and was reunited with his parents, but he felt called to return to Ireland. In 432 he was consecrated a bishop, and he spent the rest of his life in Ireland, working tirelessly to convert local pagans, baptizing many thousands of people and ordaining local clergy wherever he went. Patrick attempted to introduce the diocesan system of church organization to Ireland, but this was not a success because Irish society lacked cities to provide natural centres of government. Instead, society was organized tribally, and in this context the monasteries that Patrick founded became the central feature of the Irish church.

A final example demonstrates how thin the veneer of Christian monasticism over tribal loyalties and habits could be. Columba was born in 521 to a royal family, and grew up in a school attached to an Irish monastery. By all accounts he had a violent personality, and in 560 a dispute over the ownership of a manuscript descended into violence between several tribes culminating in the battle of Culdreihmne. This battle, which Columba won, claimed around 3,000 lives, and unsurprisingly Columba was expelled from Ireland by the church authorities. On being exiled, however, Columba and 12 companions sailed to Iona, where they founded the famous monastery. They undertook several successful missionary journeys to Scotland and the Hebrides, and he was later venerated as St Columba.

England: The ebb and flow of early Christianity

The history of Christianity in England in this early period provides an excellent case study in the patchy, fragile, and frequently checked progress of early Christianity as it spread across northern Europe. The extent to which Christianity was established in England in the Roman period has been discussed in Chapter 1 (page 6). However, from 430 for around 150 years, successive invasions of Jutes, Angles and Saxons made Christianity virtually extinct in England, except where refugees took it to the remote edges of the land, such as Wales and Cornwall. Gildas, who wrote in Brittany in 547, is our main source for this time. He was very critical of British clergy, but there is evidence that some structure and monasteries remained. Bede, writing his *Ecclesiastical History of the English People* (731), complained that the church in England had made no effort to convert the Anglo-Saxons; there is little evidence either to support or counter this assertion. But when the papal envoy Augustine arrived in Kent in 597, sent to convert England, he found a local church organization already in existence in the south of England, with its own bishops.

Over the seventh century, England was converted through the uncoordinated 'pincer movement' of Celtic missions from the north, from the Irish and Scottish monasteries already discussed, and Augustine's Roman mission from the south. The different emphases of these two pedigrees of Christianity led to some confusion and clashes as they met in the middle: this is the background to the famous Synod of Whitby which took place in 663.

The history of the Roman mission had begun some years before. For many years, it had been a matter of concern that areas in the north that had been Christian, such as England, were being overrun by paganism. Gregory (later 'the Great'), a Roman monk, was particularly concerned about this. The story goes that one day he came across a group of fair-haired boys for sale in the slave market in Rome, and on hearing that they were Angles said that was appropriate as they were angelic. From then on he apparently had a particular desire to reconvert England, and wanted to go there as a missionary. This is notable as it was the first time for many years that the beleaguered church of Rome had shown any particular missionary concern. Gregory attempted to set out for England several times over the years, but he was extremely popular and well thought of in Rome, and when he finally began the journey he was recalled to Rome within three days. Instead, when he became pope in 590, he began to buy up Angle slave boys, with the long-term aim of educating them and sending them back to their country as missionaries. In advance of that, in 596 he sent Augustine, the prior of his own monastery, with some companions, and they landed in Kent in 597.

The King of Kent, Ethelbert, had a Christian wife, Bertha, and received them with courtesy – to the great relief of the deputation, who had tried to turn back in despair as they had travelled through Gaul hearing wild rumours of English savagery! At first Ethelbert said that, while it was impossible for him to abandon the age-old beliefs of the English, he would support the missionaries and let them preach. Within weeks, however, he and most of the court had been baptized. In the autumn Augustine went to Gaul briefly to be consecrated bishop, and on Christmas Day he baptized 10,000 of the English near Canterbury.

Augustine regularly wrote to Gregory asking him questions, and Gregory's replies have survived, giving some fascinating insights into the life of the early Church. For example, to a query about money, Gregory laid down the principle, maintained throughout the Middle Ages, that the income of the church should be divided into four, to go to the bishop, the priest, the relief of the poor, and the upkeep of church buildings. Augustine was authorized to write his own liturgy appropriate for the English context, using and adapting whatever he found to be most 'pious, religious and correct' in other churches. English church structures were also in theory established at this point, as Gregory authorized Augustine to ordain a further 12 bishops in the south, under himself as Archbishop of Canterbury, and to appoint an Archbishop of York who would ordain 12 assistant bishops in the north.

However, it was at best tactless of Gregory to appoint Augustine over the heads of the existing English bishops who had managed to maintain the church through years of pagan incursions, and they understandably resented this. The pre-existing bishops refused to cooperate with Augustine on a range of issues such as the date of Easter, baptismal rites and so on, and this in practice limited Augustine's range of influence to Kent and the surrounding regions; the Canterbury and York plan remained on paper for now. He was able to found some new dioceses and saw several new churches built, but the roots of the southern English church still did not go deep and it nearly died in 616 when a pagan became king.

Augustine's mission was carried north by one of his assistants, Paulinus. He had joined Augustine at around the turn of the century, and in 625 was made a bishop and sent to accompany a Kentish princess, Ethelburga, on her way north to marry Edwin, King of Northumbria. Paulinus' experience on arrival in York was similar to Augustine's at Canterbury 28 years before: Edwin was interested, and was baptized in 627 in a wooden church specially built in York for the purpose. For the next six years Paulinus led considerable and very successful missionary efforts from north Lincolnshire northwards. However, in 633 Edwin was killed in battle by the heathen Cadwallon, Paulinus fled to the south, and the church in the north virtually disappeared in the ensuing chaos. Bede calls 633 'a disastrous year'.

When peace was restored under King Oswald, Edwin's nephew, Christianity returned – but this time it was the Celtic variant. Oswald had been raised at the monastery on Iona, and naturally on becoming King of Northumberland he sent for a bishop from there. The first to come fled in despair at the size and hopelessness of the task, but his replacement was Aidan, later St Aidan. Aidan was consecrated Bishop of Lindisfarne in 635, and it was through his leadership that Christianity was re-established in the north, though this was a slow and unsteady process. Aidan founded the monastery at Lindisfarne, and travelled throughout the diocese, often with the king, interpreting for him, and converting, baptizing and ordaining. He sent out missions all over England, as far south as the Thames. They built wooden churches, and monasteries, both male, female and double (monks and nuns together in a single monastic foundation) began to appear. The most famous is that at Whitby, where the abbess Hilda ruled over large numbers of monks and nuns from 657 to 680.

By the mid seventh century, especially as missions spread, there was an increasing clash of ecclesiastical cultures as north and south met. Not only were many details of church culture different – the style of the monastic tonsure, the way in which the date of Easter was calculated – but there was a fundamental question about authority and organization. The Roman-based southern church saw itself very much as deferring to and reporting to Rome; the Celtic-based northern church had a more independent streak, and saw authority as essentially spiritually based. Matters came to a head in 663, when Oswy, King of Northumbria, realized he'd be celebrating Easter when his wife was in the middle of her Lenten fast. This prompted him to call a conference to regularize matters one way or the other: the Synod of Whitby. This eventually decided for the Roman customs, a decision that was accepted by the Celtic side (including the abbess of Whitby, Hilda) with composure. With hindsight, this decision was important because it brought the church of Northumbria into the mainstream, allowing the remarkable flourishing of eighth-century English Christianity, especially in the north, to have a Europe-wide influence.

However, although the Synod of Whitby achieved unity, it could not achieve stability. England was still divided into a number of different kingdoms politically, and there was little organizational church structure as yet established. Considerable areas remained unevangelized. In 664, the year after the synod, the Archbishop of Canterbury, Deusdedit, died, and in the absence of an obvious successor there was a leadership vacuum. For the next five years, successive papal nominees turned the job down. Eventually Theodore of Tarsus was appointed, and it was he who finally brought lasting stability to the English church.

Theodore was a monk from Asia Minor, and he arrived in England at the age of 66, with two companions, also monks – a North African, Hadrian, and an Englishman, Benedict Biscop. When they arrived in Canterbury in 669 they found only three bishops in the whole of England, and immediately set about reorganizing the church. At a conference at Hereford in 672, Theodore won the confidence and support of the bishops and got agreement on a range of issues from Easter celebrations to the administration of marriage. Bede noted that he was the first archbishop all England obeyed. When he finally died in 690, aged 87, his legacy was a church in England that was at last both well organized and self-confident.

In the eighth century, the church in England flourished. It was in this period that the parish system that is such a feature of later Christian life and organization began to be established. Parishes were the initiative of local landlords, developing out of the feudal or manorial system of government and agriculture. Each local community was governed by the local first rung on the aristocratic ladder, the lord of the manor: as Christianity spread, typically each lord of the manor wanted to have his own church and clergyman. The earliest parish churches were therefore private, endowed and owned by the local lords who built them, who also appointed their priests. In the eighth century, this system was just beginning to emerge as and when local lords built churches, but key principles were being established. The priest owed a double allegiance, both to the lord of the manor – his patron – and to the bishop. Later ecclesiastical systems of church patronage and freehold livings are directly descended from these early beginnings. Typically, the priest was supported financially in two ways: he had a landholding to farm, known as the glebe land (usually twice a villein's holding), and was also supported by the tithe. Tithing was a 10 per cent offering of the produce of the land, and was originally a voluntary offering. However, it was too important a source of revenue not to get systematized and regularized, especially in valuable farming areas, and by the tenth century it had become a compulsory form of local church taxation.

The development and flourishing of monasteries, schools, scholarship and evangelism were also notable features of English church

life in the eighth century. The monasteries were entirely independent of the developing parish system, usually predating it. Locally
varying rules of life in the monasteries were gradually replaced by
the Benedictine Rule, which gave renewed vigour and European-
wide contacts. English monasteries, such as those at Wearmouth and
Jarrow in the north-east (founded by Benedict Biscop in 674 and
685), became renowned for their learning. The best-known example
is of course that of Bede (673–735). Bede entered the monastery at
Jarrow as a child aged seven: when the monastery was devastated by
plague in 685, only the abbot and Bede (then 12) were left alive. He
stayed there until his death, reading widely in the fine library donated
by Benedict Biscop, and writing 40 books. Most famous among these
is his *Ecclesiastical History of the English People*. Not only is this our
main source for this period, it is widely recognized as the first real
work of history, based on research and with sources often cited. Bede
also introduced the concept of BC and AD dating to England, and
wrote poems, homilies and biblical commentaries (for which he
studied Greek and Hebrew).

As Bede's story demonstrates, schools were often to be found in
monasteries and bright children could be sent there from an early
age. But schools were also developing in their own right in this
period, as scholarship and learning were seen as Christian goods that
should be spread as widely as possible. Theodore and Hadrian both
taught at Canterbury; John of Beverly, Bishop of Hexham in 687, kept
a school, and there are known to have been schools at Ripon and York
also. The vitality of the English church in the eighth century also led
to its turning to evangelism abroad, where much of northern Europe
was still pagan, as will be seen in the next sections.

The Holy Roman Empire

The area roughly comprising modern France and Germany was home
to many different barbarian tribes after the fall of the Roman Empire.
However, many of these were at least nominally Christian (albeit of
the unorthodox Arian variety). After a period of great instability
and fighting, much of Roman Gaul and eastern Germany was united
towards the end of the fifth century by Clovis, King of the Franks.
Clovis was a pagan for the first 30 years of his life, but had a Christian
wife, Clotild. In a scene reminiscent of Constantine's conversion, he

was apparently successful in one battle in around 500 after praying to his wife's God, Christ. Following this success he arranged to meet a bishop and a mass baptism in Rheims cathedral was organized, in which Clovis was baptized first. From then on, he used bishops to help administer the kingdom, and strongly supported the church, founding several monasteries.

After Clovis' death in 511, the vast kingdom that he had assembled was broken up, and a series of civil wars marked the next 200 years. Remarkably, although the life of the church was inevitably affected by this instability, Christianity continued to make progress in the rural areas, with many new country parishes being established. The monasteries continued and acted as bastions of orthodoxy as well as the resource base for missionary work throughout the period. This period of instability finally came to an end as a result of Charles Martel's defeat of a Muslim army which was trying to enter France from Spain, in 732. This not only nurtured a sense of identity among the Franks, united against a common enemy, but also inspired the pope to intervene. The pope crowned and anointed Charles' son Pepin as King of the Franks, an event that both strengthened this growing sense of unity and led to a close link with the papacy.

These events culminated in Pepin's son Charles (known to history as Charlemagne) being crowned as a new Holy Roman Emperor by the pope in St Peter's in Rome on Christmas Day, 800. The title was an inspired piece of branding, though there was very little overlap between Charlemagne's kingdoms and the old Roman Empire. Charlemagne then embarked on a period of major territorial expansion, doubling the lands under his rule over his lifetime. Conversion to Christianity was part of the price of peace for a conquered tribe, and draconian laws were often passed imposing the death penalty for refusing baptism. But this, of course, as we will see repeatedly over the following centuries – particularly as Christianity spread overseas – meant that Christianity was indelibly associated with a hated conquering power, and paganism tended to have a resurgence of popularity whenever there was a resurgence of national feeling and rebellion.

However, the impetus to spread Christianity was not simply one of conquest but was also continually resourced by the monks and clergy whose motivation was simply evangelistic. Neill expresses well the way in which simple Christian persistence and readiness for martyrdom could have a profound effect. It is notable, he says:

that whenever the Saxons rose in arms and went hunting for missionaries, priests and monks were always there to be martyred. In an age of the Church which was not on the whole distinguished by heroic sanctity, apparently men and women were always found to take the place of those who had fallen. With the process of time, the missionaries won their way. Resistance to the gospel grew weaker, and by the time of the death of Charlemagne the pacification and the conversion of the Saxons were reckoned to be complete. (Neill, 1986)

The far north

Missionaries from Britain, during the eighth century in which English Christianity flourished, had focused on areas in what are now Holland, Belgium and Germany. Notable examples include Willibrord and Boniface, both monks who went on to spend the majority of their lives in these areas. Willibrord (658–739) was a monk from Ripon, who became known as Apostle of the Frisians in parts of Holland and Belgium and founded several monasteries there. Boniface (680–754) was a monk near Winchester until the age of 40, when he began to travel to Germany to preach and convert. In one famous incident he felled a huge tree known as the Oak of Thor, in a well-orchestrated demonstration of the lack of power of the pagan gods to stand in his way. Boniface was consecrated Bishop of Germany in Rome in 722 and went on to establish and organize a church in Bavaria and beyond, working tirelessly well into his old age. He was killed in 754 at the age of 74, by a group of angry pagans, while he waited for a group of confirmation candidates.

In the ninth and tenth centuries, with most of what we now think of as western Europe already Christian, evangelistic effort focused on the far north. Charlemagne's son, Louis 'the Pious', went on to focus particularly on sending missionaries north, to Scandinavia and Denmark. The conversion of these areas is generally credited with helping to end the period of Viking raids, as the newly Christianized nascent nation states turned their ambitions to becoming European powers. Louis's contemporary biographers or publicists greatly emphasized his role as 'the converter', and made much of a high point of his reign, a ceremony in which Louis personally baptized the Danish King Harald during a reception at court.

This period also saw the dramatic northwards expansion of the Eastern Orthodox churches. Byzantine Christendom, as we have seen, was restricted on the south and east by the growth and rapid success of Islam, and also by schisms over the definitions established by the major Ecumenical Councils. (The eastern churches that separated over the preceding centuries are commonly known as non-Chalcedonian because they disagreed with the wording of the Chalcedonian definition of Jesus' divinity and humanity, though the usefulness of this terminology is now questioned by many historians.) There was also an effective barrier to growth on the west because of the increasing gulf between Orthodox and Roman Christianity. Initially, missionary expansion was not a major concern of the monastic-based Orthodox churches. But from the ninth century onwards the Orthodox Church began to systematically work to convert the Slav peoples beyond the northern boundaries of the old Roman Empire.

In the mid ninth century two brothers, Cyril and Methodosius, began to learn the Slavonic language and to prepare Slavonic translations of the Bible and of the service books used in church. In 863, with these translations well under way, the then Patriarch of Constantinople, Photius, sent them to preach Christianity in Moravia (roughly equivalent to the area covered by the modern Czech and Slovak Republics). Although their mission did not take root in Moravia – German missionaries were already active there, and were ultimately more successful – their Slavonic translations had enormous impact elsewhere. In contrast to the Roman church's insistence on Latin liturgy, the Eastern church – while using Greek within the old imperial boundaries – from the first seems to have taken for granted that local languages would be used for services as new areas were evangelized. This practice encouraged the emergence of independent churches with strong national identities.

Cyril and Methodosius' translations were adopted in Bulgaria, Serbia and Russia and directly led over the coming centuries to the establishment of the Orthodox national churches in those countries. As a result, the two brothers are not only recognized as saints but are honoured in Orthodoxy as 'equal to the apostles'. The Bulgarian church was the first to be established. The ruler of Bulgaria, Boris, was baptized in 865, and the first Bulgarian Patriarch was consecrated in 926–7, recognizing the independence and autonomy of the church there. The Serbian church achieved partial independence with its own archbishop in 1219, and a Patriarchate was established there in 1346.

The Russian church was the slowest to be established, but represents a towering achievement of the Orthodox Church. Photius first sent a mission to Russia in the 860s, at the same time as Saints Cyril and Methodosius were sent to Moravia, but progress was slow and met with many setbacks. The Russian church could not be said to have begun until over a century later, with the baptism in 988 of Vladimir, ruler of Kiev. Historical sources make much of the dramatic contrast between Vladimir's savage reputation prior to his conversion, and his remarkable gentleness as a Christian. He was noted, for example, for refusing to use capital punishment after his conversion, and is honoured as a saint. Following Vladimir's example, after his death in 1015 two of his sons, Boris and Gleb, refused to fight against their older brother, deciding to choose non-resistance rather than be guilty of shedding blood. This remarkably counter-cultural witness in the violent culture of the time and place was renowned in a similar way to that of the early Christian martyrs, and was very influential in commending Christianity over time. The conversion of Russia and the establishment of an independent church there was a slow process, but the Russian church became independent of Constantinople in 1448, and the Patriarchate there was finally established in 1589.

The East/West divide

The Eastern and Western branches of the Church did not officially begin to split until the ninth century (in a confused tangle of quarrels and disputes that lasted several centuries). However, this divergence was a felt reality long before, mirroring the division of the empire and major cultural differences between the two regions. For example, monasticism tended to take different forms in the East and West. Over the next few centuries, Western Christianity became increasingly focused on the clergy, while in Eastern Christianity the monastery and the hermit were seen as embodying the essence of the Christian life. There was also increasing divergence in liturgical practice. For example, the Eastern Orthodox Church is well known today for its devotional use of icons, and this was a hotly contested area of debate over the eighth century. Similar divisions on a smaller scale took place within the Eastern churches, particularly along language lines. For example, there was a large Syriac-speaking church focused on Edessa, the Coptic church in Egypt and a flourishing Armenian church. Initially all these Eastern churches were in communion, but they gradually broke away from one another in a series of schisms over the course of the fifth and sixth centuries.

For much of the eighth century the Eastern Church was riven with controversy about the appropriate use of icons in worship, including periods of iconoclasm (attacks destroying icons). The main agenda for the Seventh Ecumenical Council, at Nicaea in 787, was to rule on what was permissible. Although the iconoclastic controversy took in all images used in churches, there were two main points at issue. The first was whether it was acceptable to make images of Jesus himself; the second, whether it was acceptable to 'worship', or give liturgical honour to, such images. Both questions stemmed from the contradiction between such practices and the clear instruction in the Ten Commandments not to make any images of God. The first question was also a partial continuation of the debates of the past 400 years on the exact nature of the person of Jesus.

The council decreed that it was appropriate to make images of Jesus because they emphasized the reality of the incarnation. When it came to the use of such images in worship they drew a careful distinction between 'worship', which could only properly be offered to God, and 'relative honour', which could appropriately be given to such images. Icons were not simply seen to have educational and devotional value, they were seen in sacramental terms as a means of encounter with God. Although a further period of iconoclasm ensued in 815-42, this was brought to a close by the Empress Theodora in 843, an event commemorated in the Eastern Orthodox Church as 'The Triumph of Orthodoxy'. The use of icons in liturgy has remained a distinctive feature of Eastern Orthodox worship to this day.

The 787 Council of Nicaea was the last 'Ecumenical Council' recognized by the Eastern Church. While in the Western tradition the role of the papacy was developing an increasing authority, the Eastern Church has always held the great Ecumenical Councils of the Church to be of the first importance in defining the faith. Through the Ecumenical Councils, the Holy Spirit was believed to speak to the Church. From 843, with the end of the iconoclastic controversy, the Eastern Church has believed that doctrine has been effectively defined: the task of the Church hereafter is simply to preserve and communicate it unchanged down the ages. The Western Church, on the other hand, has tended to the view that revelation is a continuing process, in which the church authorities have the responsibility of discriminating between genuinely new revelation and unacceptable speculation.

This was the background to one of the major presenting issues in the East/West split, the dispute over the addition of one word – *filioque* – to the creed. The theoretical issue was the appropriate language in which to speak of the Holy Spirit: did the Spirit proceed from the Father, or from the Father and the Son (*filioque* means 'and the son')? The additional clause seems to have been first used in the Spanish church some time in the sixth century, and spread rapidly, though it was officially added to Roman texts only in the eleventh century. The Greek Eastern Church thought that Latin Western Christianity tended to over-stress the unity of God at the expense of the differentiation of the three persons of the Trinity, and that this was symptomatic of that failing. More fundamentally, however, the text of the Nicene Creed had been agreed at the Councils of Nicaea and Constantinople, and the Latin churches had no authority to change that text.

This issue became the focus for all the theological and cultural disagreements between these two branches of the Church as they diverged. It also encapsulated the growing antagonism between the two over the increasingly high role claimed by the Bishop of Rome. The actual split between East and West used to be seen as happening in two stages. The first break occurred in 863–7, when Pope Nicholas I refused to recognize Photius as the new Patriarch of Constantinople, and a council in Constantinople excommunicated the pope. The second came in 1054, when Cardinal Humbert, the papal legate sent to Constantinople to reconcile the two churches, instead anathematized the then Patriarch, Cerularius, and was in turn himself anathematized. (These 'anathemas' – statements that the other was totally unacceptable to the Church – were formally revoked only in 1965.) However, historians today see these as simply inflammatory incidents in a much longer process of divergence. The crusades (see Chapter 5) were probably much more divisive than these various excommunications, particularly the shocking incident in 1204 when the crusaders diverted their energies into sacking Constantinople itself.

Conclusion

By the end of this period, then, the Eastern and Western branches of the Christian Church had clearly developed into two individual Churches. Both were active in missionary activity, particularly in the north. Almost all of western Europe was formally Christian, and the evangelization of the far northern territories of Scandinavia and Russia had begun. The sheer tenacity of remote pioneer monks had enabled Christianity to struggle through the difficult sixth and seventh centuries after Roman organization and civilization had collapsed. During those centuries, Christianity had not been deep rooted in the West, and had repeatedly been threatened and banished to the margins by successive waves of unrest and violence.

But in the eighth and ninth centuries it had begun to flourish with a new confidence. This had some downsides, such as the forcible nature of Charlemagne's conversion of his newly conquered territories. It also, however, produced the remarkable flourishing of scholarship and learning, first in monasteries and increasingly in schools, that led directly to the foundation of the first European universities as the eleventh century began. This was the period in which the foundations of the church organization of dioceses and parishes that we have inherited today were established. As the eleventh century opened, the period formerly known as the 'dark ages' was clearly at an end, and the scene was set for the remarkable renaissances of the medieval period.

Questions to ponder

- What aspects of the spread of Christianity in this period might we be able to learn from today?
- In what ways does this chapter shed light on our current religious context?
- How do you feel about the religious disputes (a) of the Synod of Whitby, and (b) between the Eastern and Western Churches?

4

Western Christendom: *c.* 1000–1500

Introduction

The Church in western Europe in the Middle Ages is the sort of church that many people instinctively think of when they think of Christian history. This was indeed the time of knights, crusaders, guilds and mystery plays, illuminated Bible manuscripts, the Renaissance, the building of most of our great cathedrals, and so on. These centuries saw the establishment of 'Christendom' – the idea, and to some extent the reality, that Christianity and the political boundaries of nation states were inseparable, and that the legal and administrative structure of those states should embody Christian principles. This was the logical endpoint of the process started with Constantine's conversion. Yet even as this became a political reality and a fully worked out philosophy, it was being challenged and undermined by other events and thinkers. Alongside this development, and to some extent in conflict with it, went the development of the Roman papacy as the pre-eminent international religious power. The tensions and debates that ran throughout this period as a result of these two themes foreshadowed the events of the Reformation (see Chapter 6).

This was also a period of dramatic social and economic change. At the opening of the millennium, society throughout much of Europe was little changed from the basic local agricultural communities of the preceding centuries. By the end of this period, the great cities of Europe had been established, along with countless monumental churches, cathedrals, town halls and even private homes. International trade was booming, underpinned by sophisticated banking and transport infrastructures, and commercial and military confidence was such that the great European powers were beginning to look further afield for global opportunities to exploit. With all these developments came an increasing sense of a common Christian identity, especially in the face of the competing spread of the Islamic nations. This can be seen in interactions with and attitudes to Islam, Judaism, and Christian deviants or 'heretics'.

With increased wealth and urbanization came a flourishing of Christian life for the laity, from the elite art and learning of the Renaissance to the lay-led worship, social life and charity centred on the guilds of the new towns. Other changes in worship and devotional practice over this period included an increased emphasis on the person of Jesus and on the contemplation of his crucifixion, and major changes in both the physical appearance and the use of the Bible and other devotional literature.

Church, state and papacy

In 1000, secular powers in the form of local lords of the manor and local kings or rulers owned much of the Church. Church buildings were normally the result of their direct patronage, and they retained the right to present clergy to the associated posts. It was common for lay lords, rather than the clergymen themselves, to have the right to receive tithe payments from those farming in the area under their control, and to pay a portion of that only to the priest whom they effectively employed. Parish churches and their 'livings' (the post of parish priest and/or the associated glebe land and tithes), therefore, were commonly seen as elements of the lord's personal property, rather like village mills or ovens (which the villagers were required to use, and to pay fees for using). On a wider scale, bishops were usually appointed by the king, as they were often important figures in managing state affairs at a regional level.

There was little pan-European church organization at the beginning of this period that was able to challenge this concept of lay or secular control of the Church. Over the previous 500 years, after the destruction of Rome as a major centre of military and civil influence, the role of the Bishop of Rome (increasingly known as the pope) had had little influence beyond the Italian states. In the meantime, as we have seen (Chapter 3), the political landscape of Europe had been transformed from a patchwork of warring tribes into a collection of relatively strong, economically and politically cohesive nation states. From 1050 onwards, the papacy began to reform itself, and successive popes began to assert their authority across Europe. This led to considerable tension with state rulers, and for much of the rest of this period there was continual jostling for privilege and autonomy between rulers and popes throughout Europe.

In 996 Gregory V became the first German pope, and he was followed by another German, Clement II, in 1046. This gave the papacy a sudden new influence north of the Alps, which their successors were quick to exploit. Leo IX (pope 1049–54) made a deliberate policy of touring Europe, holding councils and proclaiming judgement, to raise the profile and reputation of the papacy. He especially focused on issues of reform, particularly the removal of simony (the purchasing of church positions), and the reform and regularization of cohabitation and marriage laws. These were radical moves for a pope to make, as both the payment of fees for offices and marriage customs were widely seen as matters of custom and practice, properly pertaining to the king and local lords. Interference with marriage practice (such as the radical suggestion that women should not be forced to marry) threatened dynastic interests and inheritance laws, while the removal of simony threatened a valuable source of aristocratic income and patronage.

Leo and his immediate successors were particularly interested in creating monastic norms for clergy. Clerical celibacy, though by no means universal yet, began to be promoted as the norm in this period. From 1073 to 1119, five successive popes were monks, highly unusual in the overall history of the papacy. This monastic emphasis had the effect of increasing and emphasizing the divide between clergy and laity. To some extent this was the intentional result of reforming zeal, stemming from a desire to ensure that clergy were beyond reproach and provided visibly holy models for Christian living. But it also led to increased tension with lay rulers, as the clergy claimed greater exemptions and privileges from the usual loyalties and duties of a subject. Patronage – the right to present clergy to church livings or appoint bishops – was a particular flashpoint. These tensions escalated in the Holy Roman Empire over the middle of the eleventh century, until in 1076 the German bishops formally withdrew their obedience from the pope, who responded by excommunicating the emperor, Henry IV. This dispute rumbled on for nearly 50 years, until a compromise was finally reached in the 1122 Concordat of Worms. In this famous agreement, the emperor conceded to the pope the symbolic right to invest his bishops (that is, to give them their episcopal insignia of staff and ring). However, the emperor retained control of many other important rights over the German church. While the papacy had not gained the full control it had hoped for, nevertheless such events gave it an international status and enabled it to present itself as a champion of reforming ideas.

Others also wished to claim the title of reformer in this period. For example, when William the Conqueror became King of England in 1066, he set about reforming the church himself and was determined not to allow papal authority in England. He insisted on personally investing his own bishops, and decreed that no one in England could receive a papal letter without its first being read to the king. The blurring of church and state boundaries at this period is particularly clear in his further decree, that no baron or royal minister could be excommunicated without royal consent. William also sponsored a boom in church building, such as the cathedrals at Canterbury, Ely, Durham, Winchester and Worcester. With the help of forged documents, he secured the primacy of the Archbishop of Canterbury over the Archbishop of York, to guard against the possibility of schism within the church. He introduced twice-yearly diocesan synods, and began to slowly adopt clerical celibacy by decreeing that no married men were to be ordained in the future (a decision that prompted the resignation of Bishop Leufwin of Lichfield, a married man with a large family). By William's death in 1087, the church in England was much stronger and more efficiently organized.

Thomas Becket was the most famous embodiment of the clash between church and state privileges in the Middle Ages. Becket (1118–70) was born in London, educated at Merton Abbey and Paris, and trained as a lawyer. In 1155 he was appointed chancellor of England, and shone in the role. By all accounts he was both a good and loyal administrator, and a popular courtier, enjoying a close friendship with the king. As a result, in 1162 Henry II appointed him Archbishop of Canterbury, and at that point all contemporary sources agree that Thomas changed in a way the king had not predicted. He took his new role extremely seriously, resigned as chancellor and devoted himself to the interests of the church. This brought him into direct conflict with the interests of the king. Becket went on to oppose the king in his claims for the secular courts, and insisted on the clergy's right to appeal to Rome. As a result he had to flee to France in 1164. When he returned in 1170, he promptly excommunicated several bishops who had worked with the king. The furious

Henry II demanded to be rid of 'this turbulent priest'; four knights took him at his word and murdered Thomas in Canterbury cathedral. The whole Christian world was aghast at this atrocity, and in 1174 the king was forced by public opinion to perform a public act of penance, approaching the cathedral on his knees. Becket had been quickly canonized (in 1173), and Canterbury rapidly became a major centre of pilgrimage. Stories of Thomas' martyrdom were circulated widely, and were influential in the self-understanding and propaganda of churches struggling to exert or retain control over patronage and other church privileges as far away as Iceland.

Papal authority continued to be asserted, and over the twelfth century the administrative infrastructure for effective papal government was developed. By 1130, the office of cardinal had emerged, providing administrative assistance to the pope, hearing judicial cases, representing the Roman church as legates, and taking the lead in selecting new papal candidates. The papal curia (court) had also developed into an efficient governmental department handling large quantities of routine administrative work. In around 1140, the standard reference book for ecclesiastical tribunals was produced, Gratian's *Concordance of Discordant Canons*, and the air of authority that this gave led to a rapid increase in legal appeals to Rome. The crusades (see Chapter 5) were also promoted vigorously by the papacy in this period, at least in part because of the moral authority and pan-European influence that could accrue to the papacy from their success.

The twin themes of reform and assertion of papal authority were particularly prominent in the years around 1200, under Innocent III (pope 1198–1216). Innocent vigorously promoted and argued for papal supremacy in state affairs, and came up with the most thorough justifications for this position. In addition, under the influence of the new Paris school of thought in theology (see below, page 51), there was a renewed emphasis in this period on reforming clergy to ensure that they were providing an ideal pastoral ministry. Innocent was also determined to suppress heresy, and to that end both encouraged new movements such as those started by Saints Francis and Dominic, and less encouragingly waged war on the Albigenses in France. It was Innocent III who convened the Fourth Lateran Council in 1215, widely viewed as the culmination of this medieval expansion of papal authority. The Fourth Lateran Council was the largest ecumenical gathering that had ever taken place, attended by over 400 bishops, 800 abbots, and many other clergy. It was dominated by the twin agenda of crusading, and pastoral and educational reform.

The following decades of the first half of the thirteenth century were the papacy's golden age, when its power and influence were at their height. But this supremacy was already being challenged by the continued rise of the nation states. Their further development and increasing power and autonomy, together with the repeated failure of the crusades and of attempts at church reform, meant that the authority of the pope would never again be at this height.

Social and theological developments

As European society became more stable, trade and industry flourished. Alongside these came wealth, and although this remained very unevenly distributed, an increasingly diverse artisan and mercantile class grew up between the aristocracy and the peasantry. A twelfth-century renaissance has been identified by historians, a precursor to the better known Italian renaissance of the fourteenth century onwards. In both these periods art, music and learning flourished, alongside technological, agricultural and business innovations. For example, the Hanseatic League, a renowned trading network covering much of northern Europe, was founded in the twelfth century, and new technology such as windmills was rapidly adopted, revolutionizing the production of food and textiles.

These social and economic changes led to the development of a relatively new phenomenon, towns. Previously, there had been a few cities which acted as seats of government, but the vast majority of Europe was rural and agricultural. Although large areas of rural countryside remained, these rapidly became dotted with local market towns, and larger regional centres which acted as economic hubs. For the history of Christianity, these were important for two reasons. First, the changed dynamics of having large groups of people in one place led to the rise of popular preaching and new forms of religious expression. Second, the increased specialization that towns permitted allowed theological scholarship to flourish and change beyond the confines of the monasteries.

This was an age of popular preaching: charismatic public speakers found a ready audience in the new towns and cities. Much of what they had to say was political, but at this period the political and the spiritual were not separate categories, either theologically or in the popular imagination. Relatively common themes were protests about clergy privileges or corruption, complaints about the wealth of the Church, and attacks on a range of practices, such as the rising fashion for devotion to crucifixes. Some of these preachers were extremely popular, and some of their views were radical, but they were generally accepted as being within the normal range of complaints and controversies.

However, in this context it was easy for doctrines that were unacceptable to the Church to arise and gain prominence. The most problematic of these was the rise of the Cathars, a Christian variant which claimed to have preserved early doctrines, and which was reminiscent of several early church heresies (deviant beliefs). The group started in Cologne in 1143 and spread rapidly, especially in Languedoc and Lombardy. The Cathars maintained a strict division between the 'perfects', who had full understanding of the movement's beliefs, and those who were merely 'hearers'. Their beliefs were dualistic, maintaining that matter was essentially evil and that therefore the doctrine of the incarnation was a perversion and the crucifixion could only have been an illusion.

The Church had a two-pronged response to this and other deviant movements. The official church response was to launch a direct attack on heresy. Under Pope Innocent III, this took the form of outright war. There was a crusade against the Cathars in Languedoc in the early thirteenth century, in which several atrocities and massacres occurred (such as the massacre at Beziers, in 1209). However, these brutal events had little impact in quashing the movement, and so Gregory IX launched a new initiative in 1231 – the infamous Inquisition. He condemned heresy and set up courts of inquiry (hence 'inquisitors'), mainly led by Dominican friars, throughout the affected areas. Although analysis of the historical records suggests that the proportion of convictions and executions was not high, the inquiries were so resented that in some places they were discontinued. The appalling reputation of the Inquisition is a result of the procedure used for the inquiries, which completely suspended the normal rights of defendants in a court of law, making it very difficult for innocence to be proven, as well as the gruesome punishments that were sometimes meted out to those identified as ringleaders.

More informally, there was a surge of interest in using the new genre of popular preaching to present the orthodox Christian gospel. Bernard of Clairvaux, for example, led a preaching campaign against heresy in the south of France in the middle of the twelfth century. However, because monks took a vow of stability (promising to stay in their monastery) it was hard for them to respond with the flexibility required. As a result, new orders of friars began to emerge, with the explicit aim of travelling around to spread the gospel. They were usually 'mendicant' (begging) orders, relying on donations for their support as they travelled, so as to be both visibly of the people, and beyond any criticism of inappropriate church wealth. Such individuals were initially viewed with suspicion by the church authorities, but as the need for preaching campaigns against heresy became increasingly obvious they were welcomed and guided by successive popes. By 1274, the Second Council of Lyons recognized four major orders of Friars – the Carmelites, Augustinians, Dominicans and Franciscans. Friars dominated church life and mission activities (see Chapter 5) in the twelfth and thirteenth centuries.

A second key result of the new urbanization of Europe in the Middle Ages was a flourishing of scholarship and theology. From the twelfth century onwards a wide variety of Greek and Arabic scientific, mathematical and philosophical texts were being newly translated and studied. The oldest European universities date from this period: the University of Bologna was founded in 1088, and the Universities of Paris and Oxford began teaching around the turn of the century and were officially founded in 1150 and 1167 respectively. As a result, theology was no longer the preserve of churchmen: bishops and monks were superseded as the pre-eminent theologians of the day by a new breed of academic theologian or schoolmaster. The Paris school of thought was dominant for much of this early period, shifting over the course of the twelfth century from an emphasis on speculative doctrine (for example, under Peter Abelard, who died in 1142) to the pastoral emphasis of the later twelfth century (for example, under Peter the Chanter, who died in 1197). The latter's concentration on preaching and ethics was very influential on the thought of Pope Innocent III, and made Paris a major training centre for both Franciscans and Dominicans.

In the following century, works of Aristotelian physics and metaphysics began to arrive from the Arab universities, and these too had a great impact on the theology of the time. The great clash between science and religion of the 'Enlightenment' was prefigured in the thirteenth and fourteenth centuries, as university theologians wrestled with the fact that the conclusions of reason sometimes seemed to contradict faith. The most famous theologian of this period was Thomas Aquinas (d. 1274), a Dominican who focused on reconciling faith and reason. Aquinas argued that there were natural, logical proofs for the existence of God, and that, although the natural world could be studied by reason alone, it pointed to God. In the fourteenth century, Franciscan thinkers such as Duns Scotus and William of Ockham took such arguments further. Ockham's most enduring idea is 'Ockham's Razor', the argument that where there are several different explanations for something, the simplest (for example, the existence of God as an explanation for the complexity of creation) is likely to be true.

Popular religion

For the first thousand years of its existence, the Church had laid most stress on the liturgy that went on in official church services. The social and economic changes that took place in the Middle Ages led to a new emphasis and theological reflection on the religion of the laity, and on ethics and social structures. Marriage was the sacrament seen as defining the lay condition, and the Fourth Lateran Council of 1215, along with other church legislation of the period, was particularly concerned with marriage law. In addition, codes of ethics were developed for each social rank. This is when the ideal of chivalric knighthood was developed – chivalry was a Christian ethical code for the military classes.

There was great interest in how all sorts of aspects of everyday life could be Christian, and in the late twelfth century a genre of sermons began to emerge addressed to particular social groups – knights, merchants, housewives, and so on. By the thirteenth century, developing economic systems led to new definitions of the circumstances in which merchants could make loans at interest, previously forbidden to Christians (for the impact on Judaism, see page 65). Charitable activity was emphasized as a duty of the laity, particularly the wealthy, and the upper classes of the new towns began to be urged by preachers to endow not just churches but other civic facilities such as hospitals and schools.

Guilds developed over the Middle Ages, from simple trade bodies into key centres of lay religion. The members of a guild attended regular guild services, participated in the processions associated with various holy days, gave a high priority to attendance at the funerals of members, participated in putting on mystery plays and other events, and encouraged charitable giving. It may well be that guilds can be credited with renewing lay devotion in the medieval period. Until now, the model of church had been essentially monastic: guilds were a new way of being church for the laity.

Popular religion was focused on major festivals, which were both religious and social occasions. Services were often augmented by large processions – these could be to or from churches, or around the parish or the church itself. For example, the major feast of Corpus Christi ('the body of Christ', a festival focused on the consecrated bread of communion, believed to be Christ's real presence in the church) often included a procession taking the consecrated host (the communion wafer or bread) around the fields or flocks of the parish, or the parish boundaries, to bless them and pray for fertility in the coming year. While such devotional practices were often condemned at the Reformation and later as superstitious, it should also be noted that they were attempts to relate the worship of the church to everyday life.

Other new patterns of devotion also emerged over this period. For example, over the medieval period there was a clear increase in devotion to the crucifix. In 1000, the most common illustration of Jesus was of Christ reigning in majesty in heaven, whereas by 1500 images of the crucified Christ were much more common. Along with the changing imagery went an increase in sermons, prayers and other devotional literature which concentrated on imagining Christ's suffering, and either imitating it (by ascetic practices such as fasting and extended prayer) or feeling guilty about it. This was part of a general increase in a more personal, emotional emphasis in faith over this period, which included an increase in hymns written in the first person, and a new focus on devotion to the Blessed Virgin Mary, and the Holy Family. The new friars were often concerned to promote such emotional devotion among the lower classes, the best-known example being St Francis' introduction of the Christmas crib scene. It was probably in the twelfth century that the kneeling position was generally adopted for prayer. This was the posture generally adopted when petitioning a king or local lord, so its use in prayer reveals a very social conception of the relationship between the believer and God.

In the second half of this period there was a great increase in lay literacy. This was partly a result of the trends discussed so far, and partly also due to the increased standard of living in later medieval Europe following the Black Death of the fourteenth century, which had lowered the population by around a third. Alongside this came an explosion in the popularity of Books of Hours, or 'primers'. These prayer books were previously found only in monasteries: the 'hours' referred to are the set services for the daily offices that monks attended. Increasingly, it seems, these were popular with the better-off laity, who chose to follow at least some of the monastic round of prayer in their own homes. The rich would have their own copies made, often with bespoke combinations of prayer material and illustrations, such as the famous 'Hours of the Duc de Berry' and numerous other beautiful examples. Even before the advent of printing, increasing literacy had led to major advances in publication techniques, with the use of woodcuts and relative mass-production in copying workshops, and these meant that cheaper versions also became widespread among the new bourgeois classes. Reading a 'primer' became the new standard of lay spirituality, especially for high-status women, as can be seen in the many depictions of the annunciation of the Angel Gabriel to the Virgin Mary in which Mary is shown interrupted in the act of reading her 'primer' at her prayer desk.

The Bible

Many of the trends already discussed – lay literacy, the rise of university scholarship, popular preaching – combined to dramatic effect to permanently change the physical appearance and popularity of copies of the Bible. There were four main changes, which all took place in the period between around 1150 and 1250. In the first place, the Bible began to be circulated as a single book. Most biblical manuscripts that have survived from before this period were either individual books or sets of small collections of books, such as the Pentateuch (the first five books of the Old Testament), or the Pauline Epistles. Whole volumes were only occasionally seen in a monastery or major church, and were essentially symbolic. From around 1200, however, a single Bible including all the usual books in a largely standard order became the norm. The only exception was the Psalms, which were still frequently bound and used as a separate book and so were not always included in the new single-volume Bibles.

Second, supplementary texts began to be added to the biblical books. These included prologues, material such as an alphabetic Interpretation of Hebrew Names, and glosses (commentaries next to the text). The glossed Bibles got bigger at the same time as the simple Bible texts got smaller, and it was not uncommon for people to own both. This was probably due to the new university-style scholarship, as was the third change: the text became marked up into numbered chapters and verses. Initially, a system was used in which each chapter was divided into seven roughly equal parts, referenced as 'a' to 'g', and this developed into the chapter and verse system that we are familiar with today. Before this period, those who wrote commentaries were mainly writing for monks, who chanted and read the Bible repeatedly and so could be expected to recognize at least the most important passages from their first few words. This practice is still in use today among those who regularly sing parts of the Bible: examples include the Venite (Psalm 95), Magnificat (Luke 1.46–55) and Nunc Dimittis (Luke 2.29–32). The new purchasers and users of the Bible in the thirteenth century were mainly students at the new universities, and while these were often priests or friars the old monastic familiarity with the text could not be assumed.

Fourth, and perhaps most noticeably, the Bible shrank. Early Bibles were enormous books, which rested on specially designed tables or stands. From about 1150 onwards the copies that survive get gradually smaller; by 1250 it was not uncommon for a single-volume Bible to be only eight inches high, about the size of a modern hardback book. This meant that they could be carried around, used in argument, pointed at while preaching was going on, consulted on a journey – and indeed the change was probably driven by a desire to do all those things.

The new orders of friars were probably a driving force in these changes, especially the Dominicans, who were founded in the early 1200s with an emphasis on scholarship and a special mission to preach against heresy. The new one-volume Paris Bible was the ideal book for friars: it was portable, definitive, searchable and available commercially. These features became universal and enduring characteristics of the Bible. The friars' particular concern with the fight against heresy meant that the single-volume portable Bible developed a symbolic, as well as a practical importance: it was a solid object which represented and enclosed the totality of the word of God. This concept of the Bible as a single and sacred entity is one of the most enduring legacies of this period.

It should be noted, however, that this sense of the Bible as definitive did not mean that the medieval Church always read the text literally. On the contrary, biblical scholars over this period were at pains to lay out their view that Scripture should be read as having four potential layers of meaning. The key principle was that all of the Bible must be edifying. The literal sense could be edifying alone, and often was; but when it wasn't, there were three additional spiritual senses to look for. These were the allegorical, the moral and the anagogical, relating to belief, behaviour, and ultimate judgement. One of the most influential biblical scholars of the medieval period was Nicholas of Lyra, a fourteenth-century doctor at the Sorbonne and later the head of the French Franciscans. He criticized some scholars for complicated allegorical readings of the text and emphasized the importance of paying attention first of all to the literal sense of the text, but nevertheless made it clear that the other senses could also be important, sometimes more important than the surface meaning.

The new single-volume Bibles were produced in their thousands in the thirteenth century by the new stationers' shops, copying on an almost industrial scale. Hundreds, maybe thousands, survive from this period. Unlike the 'primers', these Bibles did not have pictures, beyond perhaps the odd decorated initial. But there were also many other illustrated texts in existence alongside these working Bibles, another new genre of literature known as Bible picture books. The vast majority of the Bibles were in Latin, with translations into local languages rare and widely frowned upon. However, some of the illustrated versions were in local languages, and some books of the Bible had been translated into French and adopted by the court as texts for aristocratic reading.

The only place where vernacular Bibles (translations in the local language) were common was in England, where John Wycliffe prepared an English translation of the whole Bible in the late fourteenth century. Wycliffite Bibles seem to have been surprisingly widely circulated, considering that it was illegal to possess one for over 100 years from 1407, when the translation was outlawed by the Archbishop of Canterbury (see page 87, Chapter 7). The majority of these English Bibles seem to have belonged to people who were fairly well off – the surviving copies are mainly on parchment, not paper, and look and feel like books of hours. Many of their owners seem to have used an English translation as an aid to devotion without thinking of it as a Bible as such. For example, one surviving English text from the fourteenth century ends with the words 'here is the endynge of all the gospels, as thei stonden in the bible'. It may well have been the case that 'The Bible' was thought to be the Latin text, while translations simply helped the reader to understand its meaning. This would parallel the way in which Islamic thought even today regards the Arabic text of the Qu'ran.

Conclusion

By the end of this period, several currents of thought and trends of practice were developing which set the context for the diffuse movements known as 'the Reformation' (Chapter 6). Greatly increased literacy and developments in book reproduction technology even before the invention of printing had resulted in an unprecedented level of Bible ownership, and increasingly biblical texts – if not whole Bibles – were widely available in vernacular languages. New universities had been founded, and the new intellectuals of these universities were exploring theology as an academic subject, free from direct religious control. Some of their findings, such as inaccuracies in the commonly accepted translations of biblical texts, encouraged them to question the Church's claim to sole authority in biblical interpretation. Furthermore, the increasing wealth and self-confidence of the nation states of Europe meant that their ruling classes were coming more and more into conflict with the ever-inflating sphere of influence demanded by the papacy. In addition, long-term social changes in society as a result of the fourteenth-century Black Death pandemic had seen the virtual breakdown of the old feudal system and strict hierarchy of early medieval society. While late medieval society was still class-bound and hierarchical by modern standards, it was nevertheless experiencing an unprecedented level of social movement and what in our modern period we have come to refer to as a breakdown of deference. As a result, it was possible by 1500 to conceive of challenging social and religious authorities, in a way that would simply have been unthinkable 300 years before.

Questions to ponder

- What are the main similarities and differences that you notice between the medieval context and our own modern context?
- How do you feel about the idea of 'Christendom'?
- What aspects of the new emphasis on religion for lay people of the Middle Ages could we learn from today?
- How important were the changes in the use and understanding of the Bible that took place in this period?

5

Beyond Western Christendom:
c. 1000–1500

Introduction

By around 1050, all of central Europe was effectively Christian, and the expansion of Islam on the southern and eastern edges of the former Roman Empire had meant that Christianity, which had previously been strong in Africa, Asia and the East, had become increasingly defined as a western European religion. The next 500 years saw first the expansion of European Christianity to the margins of Europe, and thereafter a series of small-scale missionary adventures to the edges of the known world.

Between 1000 and 1500, the first theories of mission began to be formulated, though military and political power often overshadowed these. It was also in this period that some pioneering scholars and friars began the first tentative engagements with other faiths (Islam and Judaism), though again the overwhelming story is one of fear, aggression and exclusion.

The history of engagement with Islam in this period is inevitably dominated by the crusades of the twelfth and thirteenth centuries. These were a series of military incursions into the Holy Land by coalitions of forces from various European countries, and are conventionally numbered from one to nine, or from one to seven. In the latter case, the fifth and sixth and the eighth and ninth are combined; but even the categorization into nine episodes leaves out several other battles and invasions. It is perhaps better to think of the crusades simply as a century of fighting and struggle for domination in the Holy Land, interspersed with periods of relative peace and even alliances, lasting from 1195 (when the First Crusade was announced) to 1291 (when the final crusader town was recaptured by Muslim forces). The crusades were disastrous for Christian–Muslim,

Christian–Jewish and East–West church relationships, but helped forge a common European Christian identity which was influential for centuries to come.

The crusades

Jerusalem had been taken by Islamic armies in 637. For most of the following centuries Christian pilgrims were still allowed to visit, and it retained its historic and symbolic importance in Christianity. The idea of re-conquering the city of Jerusalem for Christ was a theme that simmered in the background of Christian thought for the next few hundred years, but until the eleventh century it was clearly un-realistic. As we have seen (Chapter 3), before this date there was no single Christian nation or body that had the financial and military capacity for such an enterprise.

Over the eleventh century, however, the emergent Christian nation states of the western Mediterranean wanted to establish their moral and political credentials. These included growing political powers within Italy, and the rising monarchies of Spain and France. In a piecemeal way, these emergent states began to commit themselves to campaigns against Islam. French monarchs were also showing an increasing interest in extending their influence by intervening in Spain and Italy, and gradually the recovery of Spain and Sicily from Islamic rule became papal policy. At the same time, military confi-dence and capacity was growing as political organization became more reliable, and a record of some successful conquests was accrued. The Normans of northern France had successfully invaded England in 1066, for example, while those of southern Italy retook Sicily from the Muslims between 1061 and the end of the century. In addition (Chapter 4), the papacy was keen to expand its influence as a pan-European power by uniting Christian rulers in a common Christian identity and by diverting their energies away from power struggles within Europe.

When appeals came from Constantinople and Jerusalem for pro-tection against new Turkish oppressors (the expanding Seljuq empire), the pope, Urban II, was therefore quick to respond. He proclaimed a Christian expedition for the relief of Jerusalem, at the Council of Clermont in 1095, and the resulting forces are collectively known as the First Crusade (the term 'crusade' derives from the French for 'under the cross'). The pope's proclamation was very widely heeded. Indeed, the first force to arrive on the scene at Jerusalem was the 'People's Crusade', led by Peter the Hermit, which was made up of thousands of ordinary people who had been moved by their own piety to respond to the pope's call. This ill-prepared group was massacred on arrival, but the main crusader forces met with more success. The crusaders numbered around 30,000, and were not a single army but a grouping of different forces under four main leaders. Despite some rivalries between them, and difficulties with food supplies, this First Crusade successfully took, first Antioch in 1098, after a long siege, and then Jerusalem in 1099. On both occasions the populations of the cities were massacred, the cities plundered and mosques desecrated. The crusaders then set up a feudal state known as the Latin Kingdom of Jerusalem, together with three other crusader states in the region, centred on Edessa, Antioch and Tripoli.

A period of relative peace followed, during which Muslims and Christians appear to have successfully coexisted in the region. However, it seems likely that the success of the first crusaders was largely due to the fact that the Muslim governments of the region were riven with internal conflicts at the time of the First Crusade, which had weakened their response. In the middle of the twelfth century they began to reunite, and showed their new strength by retaking the city of Edessa in 1144. As a result, the Second Crusade was raised, with the aim of recapturing Edessa, in 1147–9. This attempt failed, however, partly due to the rivalry between its leaders (Louis VII of France and the German Conrad III). This failure greatly heartened the Muslim world: this new morale, combined with the effective reunification of Islam under Nureddin and his successor Saladin, meant that Jerusalem was recovered by Muslim forces in 1187. The only crusader successes in this period were at the other end of the Mediterranean, where a splinter force joined with the Portuguese to retake Lisbon from Muslim control in 1147.

As a direct result of the recapture of Jerusalem in 1187, the Third Crusade began in 1188, primarily on the initiative of the French, German and English kings. Again, rivalries between the three of them weakened the force, as did illness: the German king died on the way to Jerusalem, and the French king eventually pretended to be ill and returned home. The English King Richard ('the Lion-heart'), with a severely depleted army, managed to take the port town of

Acre and defeat Saladin in battle. He was within sight of Jerusalem but did not attempt to attack it, apparently because of well-founded doubts that he would be able to hold on to it once taken. However, his military successes so far meant that he was able to negotiate a peace treaty with Saladin, under the terms of which Jerusalem remained in Muslim hands but Christian merchants and pilgrims were to be allowed access.

Little success was had by any crusading forces after this point. The crusading armies were repeatedly beset with internal rivalries, problems of food supply, and transport difficulties, while the Muslim leadership in the region, now united, remained a force to be reckoned with. However, as King Richard's experience demonstrates, peace treaties and negotiations remained possible where military force was ineffectual. This did not prevent further attempts at military crusades – in 1202–4 (the fourth), 1217–21 (fifth), 1228–9 (sixth), 1248–54 (seventh), 1270 (eighth) and 1271–2 (ninth) – but all were unsuccessful.

The only brief period during which a Christian again ruled in Jerusalem was as a result of the Holy Roman Emperor Frederick II's Sixth Crusade in 1228–9, and the success came not through military force but through political negotiation. Frederick had married the daughter of the King of Jerusalem, Yolanda, in 1225, and when she died in 1228 he declared himself king. He managed to negotiate a treaty giving him most of Jerusalem but allowing Muslim rule of the Dome of the Rock and the Al-Aqsa Mosque, and thus established a peaceful kingdom for about a decade. Many Muslims were unhappy with this arrangement, however, and Jerusalem was again besieged and taken in 1244, after which it was never again under crusader control.

The crusades of the thirteenth century, then, were almost entirely ineffective in regaining the Holy Land for Christian rulers. They were, however, extremely important in the history of the Christian churches, for three main reasons.

First, they cemented the growing division between the Latin Western and the Greek Eastern Churches. For the preceding seven centuries, these had largely developed independently. Although there had been some diplomatic and academic contact between them, the worshipping lives of the two had increasingly diverged. Suddenly, large armed forces were on Greek territory in the name of the Western Church, and it would have been astonishing had this not caused tensions. There is a great deal of academic debate about how much antagonism there was between the crusading forces and the indigenous Eastern Church: it seems likely that the situation fluctuated between bitterness and co-operation over the eleventh century. It is notable, however, that during the Third Crusade of 1187–92 the Byzantine emperor made an alliance with Saladin, apparently at least partially out of fear of the crusading armies. Such tensions reached a tipping point in 1204, when the disastrous Fourth Crusade – unable to set sail for the Holy Land due to winds, and unable to wait much longer due to the imminent expiry of the leases on their boats – diverted to Constantinople and sacked the city. This sealed the divide between the Eastern and Western Churches, the latter never again being trusted by the East.

Second, the crusades inculcated and developed a common European identity among Western Christians; as noted above, this may well have been a primary intention of the papacy in first promoting the crusades. It was during the crusading period of the twelfth and thirteenth centuries that for the first time medieval chroniclers began to use terms such as 'westerners' and 'Christians', and to refer to fellow members of *Christianitas* (Christendom).

Third, of course, the crusades were disastrous for Christian–Muslim relations, ensuring as they did that Christianity has been more or less permanently associated in the Islamic imagination ever since with military aggression and imperial expansion.

Engagement with Islam

Most Christian engagement with Islam in the medieval period was indeed military rather than evangelistic. The rapid spread of Islam towards and into Europe over the preceding centuries (see page 28 of Chapter 3) meant that Muslims were primarily seen as a military threat. Muslims (known as 'Infidels' in the terminology of the time) were not often seen even as potential converts, but as competitors to be eliminated or captured. We should not therefore look back on this period and hope to see sober theological conversations about the competing truth-claims of the two religions; this would be hopelessly anachronistic and unrealistic.

However, this antagonism was not universal. There was some interest in medieval intellectual and church circles in discovering more about, and engaging in dialogue with, Islamic life and thought. The influential theologian Thomas Aquinas laid an unusual stress for the time on what we might today call universal human rights, arguing that even Infidels had certain basic rights that should be respected. St Francis of Assisi seems to have been the first person to attempt to engage in mission to the Muslim world. His emphasis in mission in Europe was on the simplicity and beauty of the gospel message, and he appears to have concluded that the Muslim world too simply needed this message to be preached clearly and straightforwardly. He journeyed to Morocco in 1212, to Spain (then part of the Islamic empire) in 1214, and to Egypt in 1219. There is no record of any success in terms of numbers converted on any of these journeys, but in Egypt he was apparently received as a holy man by the Sultan, and he appears to have been both allowed to preach and listened to with respect.

Another important figure in the early history of Christian–Muslim dialogue was Ramon Llull, a prominent apologist at the time ('apologist' does not mean apologizing: it is the technical term for someone who explains the Christian faith to those who don't believe it). Llull was a Majorcan nobleman and a well-regarded scholar, and had a particular interest in studying languages. Mission to the Islamic world, and promoting engagement with Islamic thought in Europe, were Llull's passions from around 1265 until his death at the age of 80 in 1315. He founded a college for the study of ancient languages at Miramar in 1276, and in 1311–12 persuaded the Council of Vienne to establish five colleges, at the major European universities of Rome, Bologna, Paris, Oxford and Salamanca, for the study of Hebrew, Arabic, Syriac and Greek. His interest was not simply academic: Llull himself made four missionary visits to North Africa, dying of injuries sustained from a hostile crowd on his final visit in 1315. He was probably the first scholar to formulate a theory of mission, focusing on the importance of knowledge of the local language and culture, effective witness in a holy life by missionaries, and reasoned debate. These themes pre-empted the much better known Jesuit missions of later centuries.

Relations with Judaism

Alongside the increased tension between Christians and Muslims, and the increased sense of a European Christian identity that resulted, anti-Jewish feelings arose. Previously, Jews had lived on relatively peaceful terms alongside Christians once the persecutions of the first centuries had ceased. It is often said that Jews were important to the early medieval economy because Christians were forbidden to lend money at interest, whereas Jews had no such prohibition. This gave them an important economic niche as moneylenders and early bankers. Some individuals were able to become wealthy as a result, though this was never the experience of the majority, and those who seemed to be doing too well were always vulnerable to heavy and fairly arbitrary taxation. In later years this alleged wealth was often seen by historians as a flashpoint for envy and resentment, and in the popular imagination it was symptomatic of Jewish greed and sharp practice (Shakespeare's *Merchant of Venice* being a good example). As we have seen (Chapter 4) with the development of the European economy in this period a Christian ethic of banking was formulated, and it is interesting to reflect on whether increased anti-Jewish feeling arose partly from a desire to monopolize the profits of moneylending and international banking networks.

Nevertheless, it is clear that Christian–Jewish relations were primarily a casualty of the general hardening of Christian attitudes over the medieval period, in response both to the Islamic military threat and to the threat of heresy within Europe itself. One motivation behind the preaching of the crusades by successive popes seems to have been deliberately to create a sense of pan-European Christian identity, and Jews throughout Europe suffered as a consequence. It was also the case that Jews fought alongside Muslims to defend Jerusalem from the first crusaders, and this contributed to a sense of Jews as the enemy within. The first widespread persecution of Jews in medieval Europe occurred in the Rhineland at the time of the First Crusade, when the Jewish communities there were virtually wiped out.

Officially, the Church defended the rights of Jews, but in practice local feelings tended to override this official protection. In response to the persecution of Jews during the First Crusade, Callixtus II issued a papal bull, *Sicut Judaeis*, in which he affirmed the right of the Jews to practise their own religion and threatened excommunication to anyone using violence against them or their property, or disturbing their worship, festivals or cemeteries. Despite this, however, there was growing anti-Jewish hostility over the course of the twelfth century.

Sicut Judaeis was reaffirmed several times by successive popes over the following centuries, but the very repetition implies that its terms were widely ignored. Its later repetitions are perhaps less convincing: they removed some of the original protections, and other decrees told a different story. Particularly notable are the decrees of the Fourth Lateran Council (1215), which among many instructions for church reform required that Jews wear distinctive dress so that they could be readily identified – a practice that was chillingly replicated in Nazi Germany over seven centuries later.

Waves of anti-Jewish feeling and persecutions tended to arise with each successive crusade. During the Second Crusade (1147), Jews in France were particularly targeted, and during the preparations for the Third Crusade (1188) life for Jews in England became ever more intolerable. Anti-Jewish legislation became increasingly restrictive in England, and local persecutions more widespread, until finally Jews were officially banished from England in 1290. They were not permitted to return until the seventeenth century.

Many found a home in Muslim Spain, where over the later medieval period they came under attack as Christian kings reconquered Spanish territory. In 1391, many thousands of Jews were killed in a particularly violent episode in Seville, and in the resulting atmosphere of fear many others agreed to be baptized. Originally they hoped to continue being Jews under the veil of being baptized Christians, but the Inquisition was set to work rooting them out, and again many thousands were imprisoned, tortured and killed over the coming years. When King Ferdinand and Queen Isabella finally re-conquered the whole of Spain in 1492, the Jews were banished. Many fled to the Muslim world where they were tolerated and indeed sometimes welcomed: the Ottoman Emperor Bayazid II even sent the Ottoman fleet to rescue Jewish refugees from Spain and take them to safety in Greece and Turkey.

The ostensible reason for the expulsion of the Jews from Spain was their alleged involvement in the murder of a child, Christopher of La Guardia. This was simply one in a long line of accusations of Jewish ritual murder of children, which flourished from the twelfth century onwards. A similar case, that of Little Hugh of Lincoln, had preceded the expulsion of the Jews from England in 1290. There was a popular belief, commonly known today as the 'blood libel', that Jews used human blood, particularly that of Christian children, in their worship. Whenever a local child was murdered, therefore, Jews were generally blamed and became the victims of vicious reprisals. Many of these children were hailed as martyrs, and they were sometimes officially recognized as saints by the Church (as was the case with both these examples), giving official sanction to the rumours.

Missionary activity in northern Europe

Some broad changes in missionary methods can be seen over the medieval period. In the first phase, following the pattern established in the dark ages (Chapter 3), mission was primarily associated with monasteries. Individual monks or groups of monks would travel to a place, attempt to convert the ruler and gain permission to found a monastery, and would then use the monastery as a basis for conversion and training in Christianity, both by teaching and example. Both as a religious rule of life and as a practical necessity, the monks lived relatively simple lives and farmed the land for their own subsistence; this meant that they were attuned to local ways of life and seasonal patterns of living, and came into close contact with local people. They thus tended to value what was good in local customs, and often 'baptized' local holy places, such as wells, or seasonal festivals, by linking them with Christian teachings or the celebration of saints' days. Particularly in the north, monasteries were also at the forefront of valuing and preserving vernacular languages (see page 30, Chapter 3). This may well be one reason why the Reformation, when it came, was primarily a movement in the north of Europe, where prayers and translations of Bible stories in local languages had for centuries been part of the spiritual tradition.

The main focus of missionary activity in this first period, from around 1000 to 1200, was northwards. Converting the fiercely independent cultures of Scandinavia was a slow process; in both Norway and Denmark, repeating the pattern seen earlier in so many places, the ruler's decision to convert to Christianity was key to success or failure. This was the case even in these cultures where much decision-making power was effectively devolved to local democratic bodies, such as the Norwegian *things*. In Neill's dry summary, 'In most cases, when the members of the *thing* saw that the king was prepared, if necessary, to thrust his religion down their throats at the point of the sword, they saw reason; a happily democratic solution was arrived at, and all agreed to substitute the new religion for the old' (Neill, 1986). Iceland, even more remote and independent, provides perhaps the only example in history of Christianity being accepted as the national religion by a genuinely democratic process. Here, it seems that the local leaders all agreed to lay the competing claims of the old and new religions before a wise man, and to accept his considered decision. When his decision was for Christianity, it does indeed appear to have been accepted peacefully.

Sweden and Finland were the slowest to convert, but by around 1200 most of the continent of Europe was Christian, at least in name. The exception was the southern and eastern Baltic, where the Wends, Prussians, Lithuanians and others were united only in their determination never to be Christians. Despite being under considerable pressure on all sides, these areas were only finally 'converted' by the military campaigns of the Order of Teutonic Knights. The Knights were given permission by the papacy to annex any pagan lands that they conquered on condition that they provided Christian instruction to the displaced inhabitants; this was glossed as being in 'compensation' for the loss of their lands. As a result of this incentive Prussia was finally formally annexed to Christian Europe, though on extremely harsh terms. One of the 'treaties' of conquest specified that all unbaptized inhabitants must be baptized within one month, on pain of banishment: the punishment for apostasy after conversion was being sold into slavery. After this, only the Lithuanians held out, until a combination of war, politics and marriage alliances meant that the Lithuanian ruler Jagiello was finally baptized on his marriage to a Polish princess in 1386. This was an event which historians generally agree marks the end of organized or widespread paganism in Europe.

Mission at home and abroad: the Friars

In the thirteenth, fourteenth and fifteenth centuries, the great Orders of Friars dominated missionary activity. These based their rule of life not on the ideal of stability in a monastery, but in a travelling life of preaching. They were missionary by design, founded specifically in order to go out and spread the Christian gospel. This was a major change from the historic focus of monasticism, which had been to promote the holiness and salvation of the monks and their local community. The Friars did not take vows of stability, a commitment to staying in one place, which was a key feature of typical monastic vows, and at first they were regarded with suspicion by the church authorities, because their lack of monasteries meant that they were harder to keep track of and control. The major movements were the Franciscans and the Dominicans (sometimes known as Grey Friars and Black Friars, after their habits), which despite their similarities had very different emphases.

St Francis of Assisi (1181–1226), the founder of the Franciscan movement, emphasized the beautiful simplicity of the gospel. Francis is most famous for the story of his preaching to the animals and birds, a story designed to show the importance he placed on his core activity of preaching the gospel to whoever would listen. It also emphasizes his pervasive and distinctive sense of equality and belonging – brother/sisterhood, in his language – with all creation. He is generally agreed to have been the inventor of the three-dimensional nativity scene, using it to convey the Christmas story to the locals in a dramatically visual way. He is widely credited with the quote 'Preach the gospel at all times; use words when necessary': this exact quotation seems to be apocryphal, but Francis did say, in his 1221 Rule, that while only those friars who were properly authorized should preach, 'let all the brothers, however, preach by their deeds'.

It is reliably documented in both European and Arab sources that in 1219 St Francis and a companion travelled to Egypt during one of the crusading conflicts, and crossed the Saracen lines to preach to the Sultan. Francis was apparently well received and listened to with courtesy, and was certainly allowed to return to the crusader camp in peace, but only in later legend did his preaching have any apparent impact on the Sultan and his companions. Undeterred, the Franciscans continued to take their message as widely as possible, and by around 1300 Franciscans could be found wherever the most intrepid Europeans are known to have travelled. For example, there were at least 17 Franciscan mission stations in the Mongol empire by 1295, including a monastery at Cambaluc (modern Beijing). In 1323, Franciscan friars even made contacts in Sumatra, Java and Borneo.

Complementing this Franciscan emphasis on the simplicity of the message, St Dominic (1170–1221) laid much more stress on the importance of academically competent friars who could combat heresy through reasoned argument. Initially, the Dominicans focused their efforts within Europe, arguing against the Cathar heresy, preaching in towns, and studying at the new universities. But around 1300 the Dominicans founded 'The society of brethren dwelling in foreign parts among the heathen for the sake of Christ', later known as the 'Congregation of Pilgrim Friars', and within three decades had missions in Turkey, Georgia, Palestine, Persia and India. For the next few centuries, both Dominicans and Franciscans were at the forefront of mission worldwide.

Throughout the thirteenth century, occasional intrepid endeavours were made to attempt to convert the rulers of the Mongol empire that was making devastating sorties into Europe. There were some hopes that the Mongol empire might either be converted and become a powerful ally against the Islamic empire, or alternatively that the two might destroy each other leaving Christian Europe to enjoy a peaceful dominance. Three successive official envoys were sent from the pope to the Great Khan in the middle of the thirteenth century. Andrew of Longjumeau, a Dominican, visited twice in 1245 and 1249, the second time on behalf of the French king. Another Dominican, Ascelin of Lombardia, was also sent as envoy in 1245, along with another Dominican monk and two other men, while the Franciscan John of Plano Carpini was present at the enthronement of the third Mongol emperor, Guyuk, in 1246. Each reported on their return that there were a handful of Christians at the Mongol court, but each also returned with a letter to the pope rejecting any notion that the Great Khan might become Christian, and instead inviting the pope (with various degrees of implied threat) to lead Europe in submitting to the Mongol empire. In 1310, as a result of continued missionary activity, a significant portion of Persia was Christian, but the Mongol rulers were still undecided between Islam and Christianity – and soon decided for Islam.

In the records of friars describing their voyages, we are granted some remarkable glimpses of Christianity that had survived and developed in areas of the world beyond Europe, and independently of it. When the Franciscan friar John of Monte Corvino was sent as a papal envoy to China in 1289, for example, he spent 13 months in India en route and recorded the existence of a number of Nestorian Christian churches. A later envoy, the Franciscan John of Marignolli, spent a year in Quilion in 1346, and again gives us a rare glimpse into the Indian church. John's travels demonstrate how widely travelled a few friars were in this period, taking in both the Russian and Chinese parts of the Mongol empire, as well as India and much of the Near East. Other medieval travellers remarked on the astonishing rock-hewn churches of the indigenous Ethiopian church. We know, too, that when the Portuguese landed at Cranganore in 1500, they found a Christian community already there, and indeed took one of them, named Joseph, back to Europe with them. At this time the Christian church in India seems to have been around 100,000 strong, and was orthodox enough in theology and liturgy (which was held in Syrian) to impress the Portuguese.

Conclusion

Over this period Christian identity became increasingly understood as western and European, in distinction to Islam in the east. As a result, attitudes to Jews and other non-Christian peoples hardened too, and Christian mission became increasingly militaristic and aggressive. In addition, throughout this period the economic and military capacity of the European nations grew, and both missionary interests and knowledge of a world beyond Europe's borders grew with them. By 1500 the scene was set for the subsequent dramatic expansion in trading and imperial activity by the newly emergent great European powers, first Spain and Portugal, and later England and the Dutch Republic, alongside which missionary activity flourished in an often uneasy alliance, as is explored in Chapter 9.

Questions to ponder

- What can we learn from Christian interactions with Islam and Judaism in this period that might be useful for contemporary inter-faith dialogue and multicultural societies?
- How do you feel about the history of these interactions?
- How influential do you think encounters beyond Western Christendom were on the development of Western Christianity in this period?
- Which approach do you feel closer to – St Francis' or St Dominic's?

6

Reformation and Counter-Reformation: *c.* 1500–1600

Introduction

In this Reformation period the major social changes that had taken place over the Middle Ages, as described in Chapter 4, coalesced into a major challenge to the monopoly of the Roman Catholic Church in western Europe. Quite swiftly, in the first decades of this period, the religious landscape of Europe changed irrevocably. Europe was 'confessionalized', as countries and city states defined themselves as being either Protestant or Catholic. Over the following century, this change was both consolidated and extended. In 1500, although the national churches in each European country were under various degrees of independent state control, in practice there was effectively just one Church in Europe, to which virtually everyone belonged.

By the end of this period this monopoly had been shattered, and the European Church was divided along both state and confessional lines, with most northern states being Protestant and most southern states Catholic. In addition, this increased variety had spawned hundreds if not thousands of small churches and sects which dissented from both of these mainstream church positions. In most places these remained illegal and persecuted minorities. However, this proliferation led to the first stirrings, in this period, of the 'Enlightenment' view that religion should not be state regulated, and that variety should be tolerated, which came to fruition in the following centuries.

The conventional dating for the beginning of the Reformation is 1517, when Martin Luther (1484–1546), an academic monk, stuck up on the door of the church in Wittenberg a list of 95 theses for debate, all questioning the legality and theology of the sale of indulgences. This simple action became a lightning conductor for a whole variety of tensions and resentments.

The Reformation which followed is better thought of in plural terms, as 'the Reformations'. There was a great deal of variety in how different Protestant churches viewed themselves and their protests, and the Catholic position was by no means as homogenous as it has often been portrayed. However, this great variety is often divided by historians, for convenience, into three major categories.

First in this categorization is the Magisterial Reformation. This saw the development of the main official 'Protestant' churches, protesting against Roman Catholic theology, superstitious practices, and clerical abuses. These churches were supported by a range of local rulers ('magistrates' in the terminology of the time), and were mainly associated with city states in the Low Countries and Germanic areas of Europe. The best known and most widespread of these are Lutheranism and Calvinism, named after the two best-known reformers, Luther and Calvin.

Second in this classification is the Radical Reformation. This is the name given to a whole disparate range of sects, alternative churches and experiments with alternative worshipping and lifestyles which sprang up in the ferment of debate and dissent that existed at this time. Many of these were disowned, and even occasionally persecuted, by the leaders of the Magisterial Reformation because they were perceived as going too far and being at risk of discrediting the main reforming impulses.

Third, there is the Counter- or Catholic Reformation. This describes the reforming from within of the Roman Catholic Church, partially in response to the same impulses that drove the initial Reformers, and partially in an attempt to respond to the criticisms of those Reformers.

Background

There has been considerable academic debate over whether the movements within Roman Catholicism to reform itself should be described as the Counter-Reformation (the implication being that they were a response to Protestantism), or the Catholic Reformation (the implication being that they were an internal impulse that would have happened anyway). To some extent such a debate is irrelevant, as it is equally arguable that Luther himself initially intended to reform Catholicism from the inside, and only became a 'Protestant' when the

Roman authorities condemned his criticisms rather than responding positively to them. It is certainly the case that Luther and the other early Reformers were part of a movement of internal criticism and renewal that had been gathering pace for some years.

Renaissance literature of the period 1500–20 had lampooned and critiqued aspects of religion and the Church. Particularly notable are Erasmus' works, such as *In Praise of Folly*. Other would-be reformers within the Catholic Church included several religious orders founded specifically with this remit – such as the Theatines, Capuchins, Ursulines and Clerics Regular of St Paul – as well as various prominent individuals, such as Cardinal Ximenes, John Colet and Matteo Giberti. Political bodies also criticized aspects of papal policy, and in 1518 the Diet of Augsburg refused to vote the pope any money for a crusade (a startling decision at a time when Turkish armies were very near indeed) until certain abuses had been remedied.

The points that such internal critics made varied considerably, but there were three recurrent themes. First, the increasingly literate and functionally learned population of Europe was growing less tolerant of poorly educated priests whose function was simply to perform rituals. The priesthood had for centuries been predominantly poor and ill educated, and the two were of course linked: richer livings would have attracted a better educated (though probably no holier) field of candidates. The Church was plagued with too-frequent scandals of immorality, which lost nothing in the telling. Not just the lower clergy but bishops too were often poor advertisements for the Church, with pluralism (holding more than one ecclesiastical office simultaneously) and absenteeism (not living in the relevant parish or diocese) rife. The office of bishop had in many places become virtually secularized, offered to wealthy and powerful men who operated as feudal lords, receiving the income of their post while rarely discharging its duties in person. As a result, anti-clerical feeling was widespread, and often extended to all members of the ecclesiastical hierarchy including the papacy.

Second, university-educated theologians and biblical scholars were becoming frustrated by the Church's claim to decide both what lines of enquiry were acceptable, and what conclusions could be arrived at.

Third, the issue of state control over church affairs, which as we have seen has been a contentious issue throughout Christian history, continued to be important in two distinct and contradictory ways. The idea of a state-run church (known as 'erastianism') had reached its height in the late fifteenth-century Spanish monarchy. King Ferdinand and Queen Isabella controlled the Spanish Inquisition after 1478, and gained control of all clerical appointments in Spain in 1486. This state of affairs was increasingly being questioned both within and beyond the church. Conversely, other ruling elites across Europe were more and more vocal and confident in defending their rights and privileges against foreign (i.e. papal) interference – whether in marriage law, the appointment of bishops, or the imposition of taxes.

Taxes were a particular flashpoint. In this period taxation was rarely systematic, but relied on ad hoc levies to meet immediate needs, such as the expenses of a particular war. Rulers were expected to meet the day-to-day running costs of their household and administration out of the income from their considerable estates. Similarly, the nobility met the costs of governing on a local and regional level from their own resources. The ability of rulers to impose and collect taxes in this period was not a right, and taxation for major expenses such as wars was almost entirely reliant on the willingness and ability of the nobility and the population at large to pay. The ability of the pope to levy church taxes on the people – thus lessening the resources available to the king – was therefore a highly fraught issue.

Against this background of a range of critiques of the Church, the presenting issue for the reformation movement, and the impetus for Martin Luther's 95 theses, was the sale of indulgences. An indulgence was a special papal dispensation from some period of time in purgatory. It was thus a by-product of the highly developed medieval theology of the afterlife, in which a third option – purgatory – had joined heaven and hell as a potential destination after death. Purgatory was the place where the sins that you had amassed in this life would be punished, after which you would be free to proceed to heaven. Purgatory itself seems to have been an unintended consequence of the development of penitential discipline and the detailed theological thinking of the Middle Ages. The doctrine of original sin had been developed, which held that everyone was full of sin as a result of either (in various theologians' arguments) our common descent from Adam and Eve and their original act of disobedience in Eden, and/or the sexual act involved in our conception. Jesus' death was not held to be a total solution to this, because it was observed that Christians continued to sin. Penitential discipline was thus developed, and purgatory was originally conceived in this economy of salvation as a generous solution to the question of what happened to, for example, an unbaptized baby who died, or someone who died without the chance to make a final confession. The answer was said to be that they spent a certain time in purgatory, after which they were absolved. This avoided having to say that such people were automatically condemned to hell, which would otherwise have been the logical conclusion of the medieval Church's insistence on the need for the sacraments for salvation.

Originally, indulgences were awarded only in exceptional circumstances. The first known example comes from the preaching of the First Crusade in 1095, when Pope Urban II declared a plenary (full) indulgence to all crusaders. Increasingly over time, however, they were requested by and granted to all sorts of people for fairly usual Christian activities – attending mass, helping to build a new church, putting on a guild play or participating in a religious procession. Pilgrimage destinations lobbied hard for indulgences to be granted to those who travelled to them, as these could substantially raise visitor numbers and thus benefit the local and ecclesiastical economy.

There had always been question marks over the practice of granting indulgences, and the system had long been abused by pedlars selling forgeries, but the campaign sponsored by Pope Leo X in 1517 was the last straw. Leo was trying to raise a substantial sum to rebuild St Peter's Basilica in Rome, and developed a fundraising campaign in which travelling salesmen literally sold indulgences to donors. The most notorious offender was a Dominican monk, Johann Tetzel, whose activities sparked Luther's reaction. Tetzel left the financial nature of the transaction in no doubt, and Luther's 27th thesis has committed his sales pitch to history – 'as soon as a coin in the coffer rings, a soul from purgatory springs'.

The Magisterial Reformation

As we have seen, there was nothing new about criticizing elements of what the Church was doing. In posting his 95 theses to the church door at Wittenberg in 1517 Luther was following normal academic practice. Articles for debate were expected to be posted publicly, and public disputation followed. It was not immediately clear, therefore, that this moment marked the beginning of enduring church schism. However, the reaction of the church hierarchy ensured that this was the case. Instead of engaging with Luther's criticisms and questions, those who summoned him simply demanded that he accept the authority of the Church. Luther was excommunicated in 1520, by which time he had become a local hero in Wittenberg, and was protected by the local ruler, the Elector Friedrich.

The protection of such local rulers was critical in the success of the Protestant Reformation. The Magisterial Reformation is so called not because the church leaders were wise and 'magisterial' in their behaviour, but because these churches were promoted and protected by the civil authorities, the magistrates (a term that embraced all holders of civil, rather than religious, authority, from a king to a local town official). All of the new Protestant churches that emerged over the ensuing decades, despite very real differences in theology and organization, had in common their identification with a particular town or region. They also retained, in common with the Roman Catholic Church, the assumption that everybody within that area would be a Christian, and that a common Christian identity was essential for the healthy functioning of the community. An early example was the city of Zurich, which established an independent church from as early as 1520 under the leadership of another major Reformation figure, Zwingli. In Zurich, church doctrine and public policy alike were decided by the magistrates: Rome initially turned a blind eye to this aberration, because of Zurich's historical importance as a political ally. Another key figure, Bucer, presided over a similar arrangement in Strasbourg. These early 'Lutheran' forms of Protestantism spread rapidly across the German states. Anti-papalism and real religious fervour combined with the fact that religious reform was an ideal tool in the ongoing power struggles between local princes and cities and the Holy Roman Emperor. Simple economic growth was another important factor, with Protestant literature sparking important international printing industries in towns such as Geneva.

What we now know as 'Lutheranism', then, was never an entirely cohesive movement. It was based in different places on the leadership and thought of different charismatic church leaders, such as Zwingli and Bucer, as well as Luther himself. In order to mount a more coordinated defence against Catholic critiques, the Protestant rulers tried repeatedly to broker theological agreements between the various different branches. Initiatives such as the Colloquy of Marburg in 1529 and the Augsburg Confession of 1530 attempted to come up with a form of words describing Protestant belief that all could agree on. These were unsuccessful, but a more important division was about to emerge.

John Calvin (1509–64) was a French Protestant, originally a lawyer, who fled from France during a wave of anti-Protestant persecution in 1534. He became an exile in Switzerland, and in 1536 both wrote the first edition of his major work, *The Institutes of the Christian Religion*, and was invited to begin the work of reforming the church in Geneva. However, his reforms pressed for too much change too quickly to be acceptable to the people of Geneva, and he was banished in 1538. Calvin moved on to Strasbourg, where he preached and lectured daily, and his reputation grew. In 1541 he was invited back to Geneva by the city council to found a new type of church state, in which Bucer's vision for Strasbourg would be put into practice and the entire town run on godly principles.

Instead of bishops, priests and deacons running the church, and magistrates running the city, Calvin's instructions put in place an integrated structure for the running of his 'godly city' in which pastors, deacons, doctors (those who taught) and elders were responsible, in various combinations, for all aspects of both church and social life. This 'Genevan experiment' was the basis for a variety of different systems of church government tried elsewhere, all based on the assumption that church and state were properly integrated in a truly godly society. These are collectively known as Presbyterian systems, as the various committees in Geneva were often called presbyteries in other contexts. This Calvinistic tradition is also known, confusingly, as the 'Reformed' tradition, a term which is distinct from 'Protestant' as it refers only to Calvinism and not Lutheranism.

Calvinism spread widely. The Scottish Reformer John Knox preached in Geneva from 1556 to 1559, and was highly influential in the foundation of Scottish Presbyterianism on his return. It spread to France, Poland, the Netherlands and the Palatinate through a combination of specific missions and a dedicated campaign of education and persuasion. Calvinism had an influence in England, too (see Chapter 7), especially through the experiences of those bishops and clergy who had been exiled during Mary's brief Catholic revival.

Calvinism appealed because it offered a practical example of well-structured, self-governing communities, and the Genevan example showed that it could work in practice. Geneva was well known to be peaceful, ordered, disciplined and prosperous, and many sought to emulate its success through copying its religion.

Just as there were several failed attempts over the first few decades of the Reformation to reach agreement between the various different branches of Lutheranism, so many of the rulers of Protestant areas tried repeatedly to broker an agreement between Lutheran churches and Calvinist or 'Reformed' churches, in order to present a united Protestant front. However, these attempts all failed, as there were some fundamental theological differences between the two. Calvinist theologians tended to regard Lutherans as only half-reformed, while Lutherans thought Calvinists had discarded too much that was good in the tradition. The two main areas of disagreement were sacramental theology and predestination.

The sacramental theology of Luther and his followers maintained the belief that God really was present and active in the sacraments of communion and baptism. Although the Roman Catholic view of 'transubstantiation' – that the bread and wine of communion actually become the body and blood of Jesus – was rejected, Lutheranism continued to hold that there was a sense in which the elements of communion held God's 'real presence'. Reformed theologians held a range of differing views about what happened at communion, but all agreed that the sacraments were more about people doing something than God doing something. For example, the people were reaffirming their commitment to God, building community, remembering the story of salvation, and so on. This was important, but communion was not essential to salvation, as the Catholic Church believed. Reformed theologians felt Lutheranism was dangerously close to this Catholic view, and could easily slip back into superstitious practices.

The second key difference between Lutheranism and Calvinism was in their differing doctrines of predestination. For both, this was the logical outworking of the Protestant emphasis on salvation by faith rather than by works: it was not possible for an individual to earn salvation by being particularly good, and certainly not by attending church, taking communion, or going to confession. This didn't mean that what you did didn't matter; the new Protestant city states demanded a very high moral standard of living from their citizens.

Rather, what was being rejected was a caricature of the Catholic view, that you could atone for any sins by going to mass and confession frequently. The Reformers thought that the popular religion of the past was much too superstitious, implying that taking communion worked like a piece of magic. Instead, therefore, they held that God has 'pre-destined' the salvation of some individuals. However, Calvin took this logic even further and described 'double predestination', the view that some are predestined to salvation, and some are predestined to damnation. In other words, God has chosen or 'predestined' (in Calvin's most common usage, 'elected') those who are to be saved and those who are to be damned, and there is nothing we can do about which category we are in.

Some radical groups (notably the Ranters in seventeenth-century England) developed this argument still further. They argued that, as a result, there was no moral law or guidance at all for the elect, and even said that the more outrageous your behaviour the more faith in your election you were displaying. Calvinistic communities were by contrast extremely morally conservative, and it was generally held to be the case that although good behaviour couldn't be effective in securing your salvation, nevertheless it displayed it – so people were extremely careful in their behaviour to try to assure themselves and others that they were indeed among the elect. Lutheranism, and Anglicanism, never subscribed to double predestination, but maintained a belief that charitable works (but certainly not 'religious' works such as attendance at services or paying for prayers) were efficacious in some way, though the theological underpinning of this was somewhat hazy.

In both traditions, the importance of reading and understanding the Bible, and of being a good citizen, was emphasized. In services, the sacraments of baptism and communion were retained, but preaching the Bible was given much more weight. The way in which these different traditions were combined and applied in the Church of England (see the following chapter) is an interesting special case.

The Radical Reformation

The Reformation, as can already be seen, wasn't one thought-through and planned movement, but a collection of very different but related responses to the medieval Catholic Church. The Magisterial

Reformers maintained a recognizable core of Christian orthodoxy, such as belief in the Trinity and the core sacraments of baptism and communion. It is notable that even at the height of conflict between the Catholic and Protestant Churches, both continued to recognize each other's baptisms as valid Christian baptism. The radicals, however, went too far for both.

There was by definition a great deal of variation between different radical groups, and of course little or no central organization. However, there were some common themes and beliefs that frequently recur in many radical groups of this period, and they were often referred to collectively – by both Catholics and Protestants – as 'Anabaptists'. The term literally means 'rebaptizers', and was used as an umbrella term to describe any radical movement, since such groups tended to emphasize the need for adult baptism into their particular church, and rejected infant baptism. Other beliefs that tended to cluster together in such movements included an understanding of communion as symbolic only, and the belief that the church was a group of visible saints, such that election (i.e., salvation) was proved by membership. Because of this latter point the radical groups tended to be very socially exclusive, aiming to separate themselves as much as possible from the corrupting influences of the society around them. Mennonites would only marry members of their own church, for example, while Hutterites lived communally. 'Anabaptists' generally believed in a strict separation of church and state, and so wouldn't fight in local armies or take judicial oaths, and they tended to have apocalyptic views about the imminence of Christ's second coming.

The Magisterial Reformers found it necessary to reply to the challenges posed by these radicals. This necessity was partly negative, because they were concerned that the Reformation would be further discredited in the eyes of the Roman Catholic Church by association with such ideas. But it was also because such movements argued from similar biblical bases to the Magisterial Reformers, and so had to be taken seriously to guard against further fracturing in their own communities. In particular, the practice of infant baptism was the chosen battleground. For the radical Reformers, baptizing babies was part of the whole discredited Catholic economy of salvation. Infant baptism was seen as superstitious nonsense, which perpetuated false teaching by implying that the baptism had a quasi-magical effect in securing the child's salvation. They considered that the logical endpoint of the

Protestant belief in salvation by faith was that only adults who confessed a personal faith should be baptized.

The rejection of infant baptism was a shockingly unexpected development for the leaders of the Magisterial Reformation. For them, it was a basic underlying assumption that the membership of the church was the same as the membership of the whole community. The idea that adults might or might not choose to become a member was almost literally unthinkable, and they feared social chaos if this new idea of church membership being a conscious adult choice took hold. Theologically, they were also justifiably concerned that it was based on a misunderstanding of the idea of salvation by faith, making faith itself something that individuals achieved. Baptizing infants, for them, was symbolic of their core understanding that faith is a gift of God and that nothing we can do can earn it. The cause of infant baptism became a hard-fought battle of pamphlets and treatises, and as a result infant baptism rapidly became a touchstone of loyalty in cities like Zurich and Strasbourg.

Another radical development was Unitarianism (though the denomination of that name was a later, eighteenth-century development). Unitarians denied the doctrine of the Trinity, arguing that God was simply one. At the heart of this was a rejection of the claim that Jesus was God. Instead, it was argued, he was simply a very important prophet or teacher. One of the leaders of the early Unitarians was Faustus Sozzini, or Socinius, and this group were often called Socinians after him. Socinius taught that Jesus had not pre-existed with God before his birth as a human being. Another important figure in early Unitarianism was Michael Servetus (1511–53), who argued that Jesus was a union between the human man and the Holy Spirit, and who thought that the doctrine of the Trinity simply confused people. This was going much too far for the other Reformers, and one of the most shocking moments of the Reformation period was when John Calvin had Servetus burnt at the stake for heresy in Geneva in 1553, while the Catholic Inquisition also burnt his body in effigy.

The Counter-Reformation

Many of the Reformers' criticisms of superstition and corruption within the medieval Church were genuinely embarrassing, and indeed many had been repeatedly made by Catholic clergy and academics prior to the Reformation. The leaders of the Catholic Church fairly quickly realized these issues would have to be addressed if they were to counter the moral authority of the Reformers. However, a succession of weak and ineffective popes, distracted by the external threat of Turkish invasion and the internal threat of the rivalry between the papacy and the Habsburg emperors, meant that little systematic reform was at first undertaken. Luther was excommunicated in 1520, and over the following decade it became clear that there was to be a schism between Protestants and Catholics, rather than immediate Catholic reform in response to his challenge.

In the early years of the Reformation, some Catholic theologians and bishops tried repeatedly to understand and enter into dialogue with Lutheranism, in the hope of reconciling the two. However, it soon became clear that such dialogue was officially frowned on (not least by the Inquisition), and so such attempts withered away. Not until 1534, with the election of Pope Paul III, was there a pope who took reform seriously. Paul called the first of what became a long series of Councils of Trent to define Catholic doctrine in the face of Protestant critiques, and founded the Jesuit movement to reinvigorate Catholic learning and spirituality. The Council of Trent met in numerous sessions over the decades, mainly in the period 1545–63. Although it is clear that some senior Catholics at first entered the council hoping for reforms along the lines proposed by Luther, they were disappointed. Instead, the council saw its primary task as being to reassert and justify the traditions of the Church, and re-emphasized that the institutional Church had the sole right to decide how the Bible should be interpreted. The traditional understanding of communion as containing the real body and blood of Jesus was also confirmed, as were contested practices such as devotion to the Virgin Mary, the veneration of relics and the associated practice of pilgrimage.

The council did also, however, devote considerable time to trying to make the Church beyond criticism, especially in the area of clergy training. New colleges were established to train priests, and those to be ordained were encouraged to be university graduates. It must be said, however, that some of this effort was focused not so much on reforming the Church itself as on training a new generation of priests in theology and argument who could be sent out to try to reconvert the Protestant areas of Europe. Nevertheless, the spiritual renewal of the Catholic Church was given a high priority. Church discipline was restructured, and there was to be an end to absentee bishops and politically motivated church appointments. There was a new emphasis on the parish as the basic unit of the Church, and bishops were encouraged and given new powers to inspect and oversee the life of the parishes.

This period saw a remarkable flourishing of spiritual and religious life in the Catholic Church, notably with the Spanish mystics (most famously St Teresa of Avila and St John of the Cross). The original foundation of religious orders was re-emphasized, as the traditional good works that they undertook (such as education, hospitals and hospitality, the relief of the poor) served well to bolster the Catholic view that faith without works was not sufficient for salvation. New religious organizations and orders were also encouraged. The most famous of these were the Jesuits, who became very active in worldwide evangelism in the seventeenth and eighteenth centuries (see Chapter 9).

Conclusion

The Reformation period saw the confessionalization of Europe. That is, it could no longer be simply assumed that Europeans were Christians: their particular denominational identity was now in question. People became increasingly defined by the particular 'confession', or church, that they belonged to. The confessionalization of European nations as either Protestant or Catholic combined with the growing sense of national identity that we have traced over the medieval period, and with newly emerging conflicting trade and imperial interests, to produce wars of religion which ravaged Europe. Against a background of continuous tension and rivalries, particular conflicts that stand out include the French Wars of Religion (1562–98), the Eighty Years War between Spain and the Low Countries (1568–1648) and the German Thirty Years War of 1618–48. These are now largely forgotten except by historians of the period, but were both astonishingly destructive and cruel, and foundational for the self-understanding of many European nations. The boundaries drawn between Catholic and Protestant nations at the close of the Thirty Years War in 1648 have largely persisted into our own era.

This sense of religious conflict formed a backdrop to the colonial expansion of many European nations over this period, and so had a long-term impact on the development of Christianity worldwide. It is also impossible to understand the English Reformation, to which the next chapter turns, apart from this European context. The uneasy compromises contained in the Elizabethan settlement, and reflected in the current worldwide Anglican Communion, were primarily designed to protect England from being drawn into such destructive conflicts. In the event, of course, such conflict was merely postponed to the English Civil War in the mid seventeenth century. By then, however, there was little capacity for invasion among the warring European powers, and so the threat of European conquest was averted.

Questions to ponder

- How important do you think social, economic and political factors were in the Reformation(s)?
- To what extent do you agree with the Magisterial Reformers that church and state should be indistinguishable?
- In what ways does this chapter shed light on our current religious context?
- How do you feel about 'confessionalization'? How important is being a member of a particular Christian denomination to you?

7

The longest Reformation:
the Church of England, *c*. 1400–1700

Introduction

The history of the Reformation in England provides an interesting special case within the European Reformation. In some ways it is typical of much that we have seen so far. For example, the emphasis on national identity and autonomy, the importance of the local language in worship and in the Bible, the key role played by the ruler, and the emphasis on civil obedience as a religious virtue are all typical of Reformation churches. The last two of these were also defining characteristics of European Catholicism in this period. But the English experience differs too in certain important aspects from both other Protestant churches and the Catholic Church, not least in the sort of church that England ended up with (and then exported worldwide, as we will see in Chapter 9). The Church of England was established very slowly compared to other Protestant churches, with important developments from the late fourteenth century. It seems likely that this long history was a major factor in the particular form that the Reformation took in England. At the end of the fourteenth century, England was very much part of the medieval ethos of Western Christendom described in Chapter 4. By 1688, however, it had not only developed a distinctive hybrid form of reformation, but had altered its form of national government as a direct result.

Background: Wycliff

The long-term factor that made such an important difference to the English context was the history of Lollardy in England. As a movement, Lollardy was a relatively short-lived development at the end of the fourteenth century, following the thought of the Oxford theologian John Wycliff (1328–84). Wycliff had proved very useful to the king in writing a theological treatise outlining the limits of the pope's power in England, specifically on taxation. He also translated most of the Latin Vulgate edition of the Bible into English, a mammoth task which he completed in 1382, and as an Oxford academic wrote various works of theology which in many ways prefigure the concerns of the later Reformers. His thought, and the new direct access to the biblical text that his English translation provided, were popularly believed to have been contributory factors in the Peasants' Revolt of 1381. The revolt was in fact more directly the result of the new social and economic situation that resulted from the Black Death pandemic, with high mortality causing a rapid breakdown in feudal patterns of labour control. Nevertheless, the connection was made, particularly since some of the rebels justified their cause with vernacular biblical references – the most famous example being the ditty 'When Adam delved and Eve span, who was then the gentleman?' Furthermore, Wycliff's theological ideas on the nature of the Eucharist were taken up and developed by some radical thinkers to his further political discredit.

As a result, in the years after 1400 there was a major clampdown on what became known as 'Lollardy', including several executions. Wycliff himself died peacefully in his bed, having agreed to stop writing; but in 1415 his body was exhumed and hung, drawn and quartered as a posthumous punishment and warning. Lollardy died out as a movement, but the legacy of Wycliff's work was the large number of English Bibles that remained in circulation. In theory, these were illegal, but in practice the ownership and study of such books – at least by the educated classes – seem to have been happily tolerated. More than 250 copies have survived to the present day, suggesting both an extremely wide circulation and that they were neither seriously searched out nor suppressed. For comparison, we have only 64 copies or fragments of Chaucer's *Canterbury Tales*, and only one of Malory's *Morte d'Arthur*. In 1529, the Lord Chancellor Thomas More wrote, in *A Dialogue Concerning Heresies*, that English Bibles weren't at all rare. If copies were found in the possession of heretics, he says, they would be seized and might be destroyed. But other copies might be well known to the local bishop, and such manuscripts would be 'left in lay mans hands and womens' if these lay owners were 'good and catholic folk' using the text devoutly and soberly.

This background meant that the translation of the Bible into English in the early sixteenth century was neither as inflammatory nor as exciting as the sudden appearance of vernacular Bibles in other countries seems to have been. Such excitement had happened well over a hundred years beforehand. In addition, many of the arguments about the papacy and national identity had already been current in English political thought for well over a century and a half before the official split with Rome under Henry VIII (discussed below). The Reformation in England was a much longer, more slowly drawn out affair than elsewhere, and this background may well explain both its relative moderation, and the inherent tendency in Anglicanism, still seen today, to move towards change with extreme caution.

Henry VIII and the break with Rome

The circumstances under which Henry VIII declared the independence of the Church of England are well known. Henry had married his first wife, Catherine of Aragon, in 1509, the same year that he became king. Catherine was the widow of his elder brother, and so the marriage had required a papal dispensation. It was on the grounds that the marriage should never have been allowed in the first place that Henry later tried to get it annulled, after the marriage had failed to result in a male heir, only their daughter Mary. In 1529, this request for an annulment was refused by the papal court, but Henry refused to take no for an answer and appointed new advisers with the clear purpose of getting his divorce somehow. In 1533, he appointed a new Archbishop of Canterbury, Thomas Cranmer, who promptly pronounced the marriage with Catherine invalid. Under the shrewd guidance of Henry's chief minister Thomas Cromwell, various bills were passed through parliament placing the English church outside of Roman control. This had the double advantage of allowing the divorce to take place legally, and enabling the diversion of huge sums of money into the royal treasury when in 1536 the new head of the church – the king – decided to dissolve the foundations of monasteries and chantries. Henry married Anne Boleyn, and ruthlessly removed any opponents to the new marriage (Thomas More, for example, was beheaded).

It was unclear to contemporaries, and historians still dispute, to what extent this break with Rome was a Protestant Reformation.

Henry VIII himself seems to have been unsure. On the one hand, the dissolution of monasteries and chantries was justified using new Protestant theology. The logic here was that prayers for the dead, aiming to reduce their time in purgatory, were meaningless under the new theology of predestination, in which it was believed that God decided your eternal fate without reference to anything you or others did to earn it. Paying for these prayers to be said for your own soul after death, or for the souls of your family and friends, was the motivation behind most legacies left to monasteries, and was how they had accumulated such wealth. Such prayers were the entire point of chantries, which were altars with priests paid for by legacies specifically to say prayers and celebrate masses for the souls of the departed. Protestant theology was used here to justify the seizure of vast amounts of ecclesiastical assets by the crown, which gave the king the opportunity not just to augment his own income but also to exercise considerable patronage to favoured nobility.

On the other hand, Henry's title 'Defender of the Faith' (still used today without conscious irony by the British crown) had been awarded by the pope several years earlier when Henry had written a pamphlet arguing against Luther's sacramental theology. There is little evidence to suggest that Henry's private religious convictions had changed. Indeed, those keen to see a more thoroughgoing Reformation in England were sorely disappointed when the promising beginning of the break with Rome was not developed further. Interestingly, however, Henry's only son Edward (the child of his third wife Jane Seymour, born in 1537), was educated by Protestant tutors. There was some movement in a Protestant direction in various statements over Henry's reign, but it was far too little for those hoping for reformation. In 1539, the '6 Articles' reaffirmed Catholic doctrine, though the '10 Articles' of 1540 gave some tolerance to Protestantism. The least contentious aspect of Protestantism was its emphasis on the vernacular Bible, and in 1538 all churches were required to purchase a Bible in English for parishioners to consult. Worship, however, remained largely unchanged in the Catholic tradition. Henry's aim appears to have been simply to keep the traditional forms of worship and churchgoing, but under his control rather than the pope's. In this he succeeded admirably.

Rapid change: from Protestant to Catholic

After Henry's death in 1547, he was survived by his three children from three different mothers – in age order, Mary, daughter of Catherine of Aragon; Elizabeth, daughter of Anne Boleyn; and Edward, son of Jane Seymour. Each ended up being crowned in turn. Edward became king in 1547 at the age of nine, and for the six years of his reign the country was led by the privy council, under the control first of his uncle the Duke of Somerset, and later of the Duke of Northumberland. Those in charge took the opportunity to put a much more thoroughgoing Protestantism in place, and in those six years from 1547 to 1553 there were many Protestant innovations. These included the repeal of most heresy legislation, the introduction in 1549 and 1552 of the first compulsory Prayer Books in English (the second version in 1552 being a much more 'Protestant' development), and the publication of the 42 Articles of Religion (later cut down to the now-famous 39 under Queen Elizabeth I). Churches were ordered to destroy old books, pictures, statues and church furnishings that did not comply with the new outlook – orders that were unsurprisingly often unpopular, since such items frequently had sentimental or memorial value in local communities. It was clear that many items that were removed and supposedly destroyed were simply hidden away safely, or taken into local ownership, as they proved relatively easy to restore under the next regime.

While ill before his early death, Edward (or his advisers) had attempted to secure a Protestant line of succession by naming his cousin, Lady Jane Grey, as his heir. However, this rapidly proved unacceptable to the country, when there were two direct heirs already clearly at hand in his sisters. Those who had been most uncomfortable with the speed of the Protestant Reformation under Edward also no doubt saw their chance to claw back some territory by supporting Mary's much stronger claim to the throne. Queen Mary (who reigned from 1553 to 1558) threw herself into the task of re-establishing Roman Catholicism. It is hard not to see some psychology at work here as well as true religious conviction: after all, her father's rejection of both herself and her mother had been her primary experience of Henry's 'reformation'.

Not every element of the past could be easily undone. For example, it was never even proposed that the monasteries and chantries, dissolved by Henry VIII, might be refounded. It would simply have been prohibitively expensive even to begin, and the members of the nobility who had been granted monastery lands and buildings had no intention of returning them. But Mary quickly restored earlier official doctrine, replacing the Protestant 42 Articles with the 1539 6 Articles of Religion (in the process, making all the clergy who had married redundant). She also brought back the heresy laws. These latter were then used to unprecedented effect over the next few years, as over 280 prominent Protestants were killed, mainly by burning at the stake. Even Catholic observers thought this unwise, and warned that it was likely to cause widespread discontent. Foxe's *Book of Martyrs*, describing the deaths of those persecuted under Mary, remained a bestseller for decades, and firmly established both Mary's reputation as 'Bloody Mary', and a deep distrust of Roman Catholicism in England which persisted well into the twentieth century. In addition, Mary insisted on marrying the Catholic Prince Philip of Spain, a move greatly distrusted by parliament and the nobility, who feared that England would come under Spanish control. The accession of her sister Elizabeth on Mary's death was therefore greeted with widespread relief.

The Elizabethan Settlement

What we most commonly think of today as the establishment of the Church of England is the compromise that Elizabeth established early in her reign: the 'Elizabethan Settlement'. This was a very conscious political act of compromise, but it worked and it has endured. Elizabeth faced problems from both Catholics and Protestants on her accession in 1558, both of whom she feared primarily as political, rather than religious threats. The Catholic threat included the bishops appointed by Mary and some major Catholic families in England, but much more important than these were external Catholic powers. Invasion by either France or Spain was seen as a major threat, and this was compounded by the presence of the Catholic Queen Mary Stuart in Scotland. Mary Queen of Scots was allied with France through her marriage, and had a close claim to the English throne. There was a serious fear for many years that France would invade England across the Scottish border, under the pretext of putting Mary on the English throne. The Protestant threat to the stability of Elizabeth's reign came mainly from those clergy and bishops who had been exiled during Mary's reign, and had thus been exposed to Calvinism in Geneva and elsewhere. They now returned, full of reforming zeal, and expected to be rewarded for their loyalty under persecution.

In addition to these opposing religious tensions, Elizabeth faced other threats to the stability and safety of her rule. There were question marks over her ability to lead as a woman: Mary had been the first female English monarch, and the experiment was not generally viewed as a success. Financial issues were always a concern for monarchs, and the ever-present balancing act of European foreign policy was particularly tense in the sixteenth-century context of inter-European religious wars. There was also major public concern over who and when Elizabeth might marry, and the dynastic implications. A religious settlement was urgently needed, as the religious ferment in Europe together with the legacy of the Marian persecutions in England meant that the state of religion in the country was the most likely flashpoint for rebellion or war.

Elizabeth took swift action, securing two key Acts of Parliament in 1559. The Act of Supremacy re-established the crown as the head of the Church of England, as under Henry VIII. The Act of Uniformity required the use of the revised and reissued Book of Common Prayer in all churches in England, and prescribed a moderately Protestant style of worship. These Acts were followed in 1563 by the publication of the 38 Articles (revised up to 39 in 1571), and the requirement that all clergy subscribe to them. The articles were based on the 42 Articles written in Edward's reign, but were moderated. For example, a condemnation of the Catholic idea that the elements of communion became Christ's body and blood was removed, as were various clauses relating to correct beliefs about what happened to the soul after death. Elizabeth's motives were clear: compromise in the name of unity and political stability. The settlement effectively prescribed the continuation of traditional appearances: vestments were still to be worn, church government was to remain with clergy and bishops, much traditional church decoration could remain. The theology of the liturgy in the Book of Common Prayer was essentially Protestant – though the very existence of a set liturgy was considered by some to be dangerously Catholic. The settlement was ambiguous on crucial points, such as the nature of the Eucharist. At this stage, too, nothing was done to address the perennial issue of low standards in the church. In England as elsewhere, pluralism and non-residency were common among the clergy. Many clergy continued to be ill educated, a particular issue in Protestantism with its emphasis on preaching rather than ritual.

Initially, it seemed that this uneasy settlement might fall apart under pressure from both Catholic and Puritan (extreme Protestant) objectors. In the Northern Rebellion of 1569, Catholic sympathizers came together with support from Scotland and France to attempt to put Mary Queen of Scots on the throne. In the aftermath of this, the pope excommunicated Queen Elizabeth in 1570. The situation worsened over the next decade, particularly after 1580 when Jesuits began to enter England to strengthen Catholic opposition. There were several plots to assassinate Elizabeth over the period 1571 to 1586. In 1585, war broke out with Spain, with the declared Spanish aim of regaining England for Catholicism. However, this had the unintended consequence of neutralizing the Catholic threat within England. Nobody wanted a Spanish conquest. War with Spain crystallized the question of loyalty to faith or crown, and when Elizabeth addressed the troops drawn up to repel the Spanish Armada at Tilbury in 1588, prominent members of Catholic noble families were conspicuously present with their retainers.

The pressures from Puritan objectors to the settlement were at least as much of a threat to the unity of the church (and thus the stability of English society) in these first few decades. Puritans objected strongly to the maintenance of the appearances of traditional religion; to the provision of a prescribed liturgy (preferring extempore prayers and preaching); and sometimes even to having church government ordered by bishops and the Queen (preferring individual congregations to be given their freedom).They were particularly strong in London and the south-east, and were often in prominent and influential positions. Because so many of Mary's bishops had to be replaced on Elizabeth's accession, many of the Marian exiles held these positions and so were at the heart of the church. They were also prominent among the aristocracy (including some members of the privy council) and the gentry (including some members of parliament), and in the universities, especially Cambridge.

However, their effectiveness was hampered by the fact that they had no unity or organization, often differed among themselves, and had no single figurehead or leader. For example, in 1571 an MP called

Norton tried to steer some modest reforms through parliament, but his hopes were dashed when another MP, Strickland, attempted to replace the Prayer Book at the same time. As a result, Elizabeth vetoed any further discussion of religious matters by parliament. Puritans also shared with Catholic objectors the disadvantage of being on the wrong side of the law, and the presence of some extreme views, widely disseminated through pamphleteering, seems to have alienated moderate support. The best example of this is the 'Martin Marprelate Tracts' of 1588, a series of scurrilous attacks by the pseudonymous author on the bishops of the Church of England. These were so insubordinate that they succeeded in alienating the members of the privy council, such as Lord Burghley, who until that point had given crucial support and shelter to Puritans.

By the end of the 1580s, partly due to this alienation of aristocratic and moderate support, the Puritan movement was waning. The surviving records of one Puritan group that met regularly, the Dedham Classis, show that they held their last meeting in June 1589. Like the waning of the Catholic threat, the war with Spain and the threat of invasion posed by the Armada also had its effect on Puritans, forcing them to choose their loyalties. But it seems likely that the developing Church of England had also had a positive effect, gaining a wide base of loyalty and affection throughout the country. Elizabeth's intransigence certainly helped the Church of England to become established by refusing to countenance any alternatives. But the growing affection in which it was held also has much to do with the actions of certain prominent churchmen.

Elizabeth's third archbishop, John Whitgift, put many minor reforms in place, such as insisting that candidates for ordination show some evidence of good character and adequate learning, and that clergy could not hold more than one living simultaneously if they were more than 30 miles apart. The publication of the *Book of Homilies* in 1563 provided set sermons to be read in rotation by all clergy (except those few given special licences to preach their own sermons); this both did much to educate the laity in the principles of the Elizabethan church, and ensured that even uneducated clergy taught the church's official doctrine. The maintenance of a traditional appearance of worship did much to reconcile most people to the new theological content, while those who disliked a set prayer book were at least mollified by the Protestant theology of its prayers and of the homilies.

The early seventeenth century

By the end of Elizabeth's reign, in 1603, the Prayer Book and settlement seem to have been widely accepted and even held in affection. However, those who desired a more thoroughgoing Calvinist Reformation were still vocal. When Elizabeth's successor James came to the throne, they were hopeful. James was already King of Scotland, where the established church was Presbyterian, without bishops or prayer book, and so he was thought likely to be sympathetic. A petition was sent to him signed by many leading Puritan ministers (perhaps as many as a thousand in total), asking for reform. In response, James held a conference at Hampton Court in 1604 to discuss the issues raised. However, the outcome disappointed those hoping for radical change. The Prayer Book, the organization of the church under bishops, and most of the outward forms of worship were to remain unaltered, since James shrewdly felt that upheaval would be more divisive than worthwhile. He did, however, authorize the preparation of a new English translation of the Bible – the now-famous 'King James' (strictly speaking, the 'Authorized') Version. For the first two decades of the seventeenth century, then, church life continued much as before in England.

Politically, however, events in Europe were once again beginning to cause problems. On the continent the beginning of the complex and destructive 'Thirty Years War' between Catholic and Protestant powers cemented the 'confessionalization' of Europe. It also made James increasingly keen to arrange a dynastic marriage between his son and the Spanish infanta (princess), to neutralize the threat of a Spanish invasion. This was an extremely unpopular policy in Britain, however, as Spain was distrusted and seen as both a political and a religious enemy. This disagreement led to increasing tension between the king and the House of Commons over their respective roles in government and policy making. These tensions were exacerbated because there was a growing current of political thought in elite European circles that held that kings should have absolute authority, as God's vice-regents on earth, and James subscribed to this view. Indeed, he had written two books about it, *The True Law of Free Monarchies* (1597) and *Basilikon Doron* (1598).

Tension between king and parliament escalated after James' son Charles became king in 1639. In the first place, Charles I was expensive. He broke the unwritten first rule of kings that they should 'live of their own' – in other words, that they should use their own extensive lands and income to pay for their normal living and court expenses, only raising general taxations in times of war or other national crisis. Instead, Charles imposed a great deal of unpopular taxation, often of dubious legality. He also continued the trend established by his father towards an extremely high view of kingship, and infuriated the gentry and nobility by refusing to call parliaments to advise him. In addition, his religious views caused great consternation. Charles was married to a Roman Catholic, Henrietta Maria, and he had a great liking for high church ritual. In 1633 he appointed William Laud to the post of Archbishop of Canterbury, an inflammatory move. Laud shared Charles' religious preferences and came close to making them official church policy, encouraging medieval-style ornamentation of churches and ritual, to the horror of the majority of the population who were, whatever their religious differences, vehemently anti-Catholic.

The English Civil War

All of these factors combined in the coming of the English Civil War (1642–51), in which it is impossible to untangle political, economic and religious factors. It was also entwined with other wars in Scotland and Ireland, the first occasioned by a heavy-handed attempt to impose the Book of Common Prayer on the Church of Scotland, the latter initiated by Catholics hoping to gain political freedom by taking advantage of the Protestant infighting on the mainland. Although not all supporters of the king agreed with his policies – many heartily disliked them but simply felt that it was illegal and improper to rebel against God's anointed ruler – the Puritan influence was particularly strong in the Parliamentary army, and the question of control over the church was clearly at stake.

Charles I was executed in 1649, and the Commonwealth period of the next decade saw Puritans clearly in charge. Bishops, and the Book of Common Prayer, were banned. Towards the end of the 1650s, the strict Puritanism of the army that was in ascendancy went even further, notoriously banning such inappropriate behaviour as maypole dancing and keeping Christmas as a holiday: shops were commanded to open on Christmas Day, though only a few complied. It is clear from many surviving spiritual journals and personal sermon notes from the period that many of the population embraced this new regime with enthusiasm. It is also clear that others tried to quietly evade the new rules. For example, John Evelyn's diary records that on Christmas Day 1657 he attended a communion service in London which was raided. Listening to a sermon was permissible, but the authorities had clearly been tipped off and waited to see if any celebration of the day as a holy day was to ensue: 'Sermon ended, as [the priest] was giving us the Holy Sacrament the chapel was surrounded with soldiers; and all the communicants and assembly surprised and kept prisoners by them' (De la Bedoyere, 2004, p. 105).

There was a great deal of religious experimentation over this period, with radical groups such as the Diggers exploring alternative societal structures such as communal living. Some even experimented with female leadership and radically equal gender relations, but this was an idea whose time had not yet come. The growth of the Baptist and Quaker denominations dates from this period. Such alternative expressions of religion were broadly tolerated by the Commonwealth. However, this toleration was not universally popular. Many felt that the reported antics of groups such as the Ranters (who claimed that Christ had superseded the Law and thus anything was permissible – and who reportedly felt the need at times to demonstrate this freedom in dramatically scandalous ways such as running down the street naked), or the Quakers (officially known as Friends, and who distinctively refused to adhere to societal norms such as recognizing social superiors), were a disgrace. Colonists in the Americas, who were broadly supportive of the Commonwealth, consistently refused to adopt its policy of religious toleration and were often vocal in their disapproval.

Restoration and Glorious Revolution

After the death of Oliver Cromwell in 1658, the Commonwealth regime had drifted on, but the population was tired of fighting and austerity. Puritan influence declined over the 1650s, while the importance of trade and commercial interests for determining foreign and home policy continued to grow. The mood in the country was thus increasingly in favour of a stable and permanent order.

This found expression in the Restoration of the monarchy in 1660, with the coronation of Charles II, the son of Charles I. Since his father's arrest and execution, the younger Charles had been living in exile in France, and when he docked in England and proceeded to London he was entirely unopposed. The restoration of the Church of England, bishops and the Book of Common Prayer swiftly followed. Although many in the church hoped to be able to create a new, compromise Book of Common Prayer which had been changed in a more Protestant direction, they were disappointed. The 1662 version (the version that is familiar today) made only minor changes to the main services, though it added considerable tranches of royalist material such as commemorations of the gunpowder plot, of Charles I's 'martyrdom', and of Charles II's restoration. There is no evidence of any widespread opposition to the reintroduction of the Book of Common Prayer in parish churches across England. Rather, it seems to have been quietly accepted in most places, and indeed historians are uncertain as to what extent it ever actually went out of use in rural areas.

The lack of opposition to Charles' restoration was helped by his clear statement in the Declaration of Breda (made in 1660 before his arrival in England) that he would allow freedom of worship to dissenters from the official Church of England, along with the promise of a general pardon for the Civil War. This was later modified by parliament, who were not at all keen on the idea of freedom of worship for Catholics, but Protestant dissenters were to be allowed. The Toleration Act of 1689 allowed freedom of worship to Nonconformists so long as they were prepared to swear to the Acts of Allegiance and Supremacy (to ensure they were loyal) and reject transubstantiation (to ensure they weren't Catholic). The Act explicitly did not apply to Catholics or Unitarians, and it was restricted to allowing freedom of worship, not other legal and political rights. Dissenters from the Church of England were still, for example, excluded from the universities, or from holding political offices. Nevertheless, the Church of England never again claimed a monopoly on the religious life of the nation.

A further crisis came towards the end of Charles II's life. His brother and heir James was Catholic, and it became clear both that another heir was unlikely to be born, and that James had no intention of converting to English Protestantism. This led to considerable heartsearching among English politicians and church leaders.

Many believed absolutely in the divine right of kings; that rulers were appointed by God as his deputies on earth and were to be obeyed. However, most also believed absolutely that Protestantism was God's plan for the world and that Roman Catholicism must be resisted at all costs. Between 1679 and 1681, in the Succession Crisis, it seemed possible, even likely, that James would be excluded from succeeding to the throne, but Charles II managed to avert this possibility through political manoeuvring.

On his accession to the throne in 1685, however, James proved less adept than his brother at playing the political game, and promoted Catholic interests too far for most to stomach. In 1688, William of Orange (who was already a major leader of European Protestantism against the French Catholic dynasty) and his wife Mary (who until the birth of James' son had been the heir to the throne) were quietly invited to assume power, in a bloodless and unopposed invasion that became known as the 'Glorious Revolution'. This led to one of the largest conscientious splits of the church in England. Those bishops and clergy who maintained that they couldn't take an oath of obedience to William and Mary because it meant breaking their oath to James resigned in protest. These were known as the non-jurors, and they included many prominent and well-regarded churchmen, led by the Archbishop of Canterbury, William Sancroft. Over 400 clergy, including nine bishops, were deposed as a result. The Non-Juring Church at first seemed as if it might flourish as an alternative to the established Church of England, but it foundered over splits in later decades, and its fortunes waned as the chances of the Stuart dynasty being re-established faded.

Conclusion

Finally, then, by the end of the seventeenth century, the Church of England had come to the end of its protracted internal negotiations about what sort of Reformation this was to be. Henry VIII and Elizabeth I would have recognized immediately its episcopal organization and its combination of broadly Catholic liturgy and Protestant doctrine, but would no doubt have been appalled by its newly tolerant approach to religious diversity. This new glimpse of tolerance, however, was to be a key element of the developing Enlightenment and a key marker of the modern Church.

Questions to ponder

- How well do you think the Elizabethan settlement worked in its historical context?
- What elements of Elizabeth's settlement are still most useful today? Are there any elements that are less useful?
- How do you feel about the way in which political as well as religious issues formed the Church of England?
- What can we learn from the English Civil War and later seventeenth-century developments?

8

The modern period: *c.* 1700–1900

Introduction

The period between 1700 and 1900 saw the political and religious climate of Europe and the Americas changed almost beyond recognition. The colonial expansion of the major European powers, which had begun in the late sixteenth century, first developed into global colonial domination, and also changed with American independence. This chapter will focus on events in Europe and North America, but it must be remembered that the history of Christianity in this period is one of global expansion. Many of the events and trends discussed here had implications worldwide, due to the colonial and missionary impulses which were entwined in a close but ambivalent relationship over these centuries. The globalization of Christianity is discussed in the following chapter, but must not be forgotten in understanding the context of Christianity in this period.

Within Europe, developments in science and learning led to industrialization and urbanization, as well as intellectually to the Enlightenment. Together, these changed traditional ways of life for ever, and also had major impacts on both politics and the churches. This was a revolutionary period, socially, economically and politically. Between 1700 and 1900 there was a general fear among the upper classes that unpredictable economic, intellectual and demographic changes would bring both cultural change and political and social unrest. Many of these fears were valid and were realized: events such as the French Revolution confirmed the worst fears of the aristocracy elsewhere. There were thus two major and opposing currents of thought during this period, the revolutionary and the conservative. The general response of the Church was conservatism in the face of all these changes, which were seen as deeply threatening to the centuries-old assumptions of Christendom. This conservatism meant that by the end of this period the Church was widely seen within Europe as being out of touch with modern life, essentially old-fashioned and opposed to science and progressive ideas.

Religious revival

Spiritually, the eighteenth and nineteenth centuries are notable for a broad range of revival movements which gained considerable popular support. These popular outpourings of religious fervour stand in partial contrast to a trend to anti-clericalism in this period, but also spurred on that trend by emphasizing divine revelation and individual experience. This trend to revival took a number of different forms. There was a wide variety of small charismatic sects, similar to those that had flourished in the experimental period of the English Civil War. In addition, this period saw a major and widespread trend towards evangelicalism or pietism in religion, across both national and denominational boundaries. This trend was especially influential in creating the nineteenth-century English 'Victorian' ethos, in the pietist strand in German Lutheranism, and in inspiring many of the major missionary endeavours of this period.

In North America, the period became known as a time of 'Great Awakenings'. Over these centuries thousands of itinerant preachers and evangelists travelled far and wide, attracting great crowds with a distinctive emphasis on personal and emotional conversion and spiritual renewal. Historians generally see several waves of such 'Awakenings' as having taken place: the first around 1720–50, the second around 1800–70, and a third around 1880–1910. All were characterized by emotional preaching, often in large open-air meetings, and the subsequent creation of many new denominations.

The most famous early preacher associated with the American revival was Jonathan Edwards, a Congregationalist Puritan who preached in the Massachusetts area in the 1730s and 1740s. Before this period, preaching had tended to be a scholarly affair; the new preaching style aimed to inspire rather than to inform. (A historical parallel can be seen with the new preaching orders of friars that developed in the thirteenth century, particularly that of St Francis, as discussed in Chapter 5.) With the benefit of hindsight, this change can be seen to have been part of a broader cultural trend towards romanticism and individualism: over this period, emotion and individual response were given increasing emphasis in poetry, art, science and politics, as well as in religion.

The revivals were not part of an organized movement, but were instead a series of uncoordinated initiatives by individual evangelists. They were reacting against churches which in the American context were increasingly seeming stuffy and old-fashioned, but more positively were also responding to the particular missionary situation of North America. As American pioneers spread west, new forms of evangelism were developed to reach them, notably the camp meeting – a several-day-long gathering with several preachers, musicians and so on. Word would spread and isolated pioneers would gather at the appointed time and place for a few days of social as well as religious refreshment – rather like a modern-day summer festival, and perhaps derived from similar events in the sparsely populated areas of Scotland from which some settlers came. These meetings often inspired those who had attended to establish new churches when they returned to their frontier homes. Often these were intended to be non-denominational, but in practice they contributed to a unprecedented proliferation of new denominations in these years. This in turn contributed to a view of denominations as competitors in a marketplace for converts, often the opposite of the pious intention behind the founding of each new 'non-denominational' church.

Revivalist movements such as these were not confined to the North American context. In England, the most obvious example is Methodism. This developed from the 'Holy Club' established at Oxford in 1729 by John and Charles Wesley and their friends, which sought to help its members to grow in faith by meeting weekly to share their stories, confess sins, and discuss the Bible. Mocked by contemporaries as overly methodical, the term 'Methodist' was soon adopted. The Wesley brothers and their associates soon became extremely well known for their itinerant and apparently tireless preaching around the country. This preaching often took place in the open air, since they were usually banned from meeting in churches: open-air preaching also had the major advantages that it set no limits on the numbers that could attend, and made it clear that the lower classes were welcome.

Methodism was intended as a revival movement within the Church of England, rather than as a new denomination. John Wesley's diaries, written in code, have recently been translated and make it clear that he was very worried by the prospect of Methodism splitting from the Church of England. As a result, Methodism only formally became a separate denomination in England after his death in 1791, though from the 1760s onwards independent Methodist evangelists had established distinctively Methodist congregations in America.

A very different manifestation of revival in England was the 'Oxford' or 'Tractarian' Movement of the mid nineteenth century. This was the religious equivalent of the romantic movement in the arts, which reacted against the perceived ugliness and loss of tradition inherent in industrialization with a pastoral and quasi-medieval idyllicism. The Oxford Movement combined this impetus with a reaction against the growing evangelical influence in the church, to call both for the revival of lost medieval beauty and mysticism in worship, and for the recovery of a sense of continuity between the Church of England and the medieval Catholic Church. The movement began with a series of 'Tracts for the Times' (hence the term 'Tractarianism'), published between 1833 and 1841. Many of these were written by the clergyman John Henry Newman, who later famously converted to Roman Catholicism.

The immediate impetus for the Oxford Movement sounds remarkably contemporary. There was a fear around that the church was subject to the forces of secularization, and this was particularly focused in 1832 when the government decided (as part of the parliamentary Reform Act) to reduce the number of Irish bishops sitting in the House of Lords to ten. Condemned by John Keble, one of the leaders of the Oxford Movement, as 'national apostasy', this confirmed the growing belief of those who became the movement's leaders both that the world was leaving faith behind, and that worship had become so 'plain' that it was failing to attract people back.

The Romanizing aspects of the Oxford Movement – such as the revival of vestments, or candles on the altar – were widely condemned, and some priests ended up in court or in prison as a result. Nevertheless, the movement had a long-term impact on the worship of the Church of England. It shone a spotlight on liturgical practice and raised questions about why and how we do things, and their emotional and spiritual impact on worshippers, which are still very much at the forefront of church thinking on liturgy.

It also fed into the Parish Communion movement of the early twentieth century. Until the 1960s and 1970s, the main service in most Church of England churches was the Book of Common Prayer service of Matins, with the communion service happening separately (this is why so many Church of England churches continue to have the '8 a.m.' and the '10 a.m.' congregations, even when both services are now eucharistic). The relatively widespread use of vestments, candles, and things like processions and robed choirs in even 'middle of the road' Anglican churches is testament to the impact of the movement. Most Church of England services today would look oddly Catholic to a visitor from the eighteenth or early nineteenth century.

Enlightenment and religious toleration

The widespread fear and loathing that the Oxford Movement's attempts to revive traditional Catholic forms of worship aroused demonstrate how far from being a religiously tolerant society England was in the early nineteenth century. Nevertheless, the development of toleration was an important feature of the modern period. During the establishment of the Church of England in the late sixteenth and early seventeenth centuries, it was explicit that a key aim was to achieve unity of practice, civil obedience and thus peace. Dissent from the established church was therefore seen as treason, rather than heresy. One of the key changes of the later seventeenth and eighteenth centuries was the development of theories of toleration, and in practice an acceptance that other denominations existed. England was by no means alone in this respect. Until the late seventeenth century, in most countries throughout Europe, and in parts of the new world such as the Catholic areas of South America, there were no such things as denominations recognized – there was simply the established church, and dissenters were marginalized at best, persecuted at worst.

However, in the seventeenth century the concept of religious toleration became a hot topic of debate. In France, for example, the Edict of Nantes at the end of the French Wars of Religion in 1598 had granted a certain measure of toleration to Protestants by deliberately separating out civil and religious unity. When this was repealed by Louis XIV in 1685 the renewed persecutions that followed led to around 150,000 French Protestants leaving the country, and a great deal of pamphleteering followed. At the same time new societies in America were being formed, and were having to learn to live with huge religious diversity, though at this early stage some were still hoping to win over all to their point of view. Some (famously the Roman Catholic Jesuit missionaries) were even beginning to think about the other faiths that they encountered in mission as perhaps worthy of engagement in discussion rather than simply suppression, though this remained a minority viewpoint. In addition, the growing number and influence of revival movements in Europe and America over the following century further undermined the concept of an official state church, with rapidly rising numbers of new denominations and their adherents.

Toleration was being debated academically too, and was a key feature of the cultural and philosophical movement known as the Enlightenment. This diffuse movement brought together developing interests in science and philosophy with political theory, and had a particular interest in ideas around human rights and natural law. The latter was a new emphasis, partly inspired by scientific developments, on what was natural rather than on what was divinely ordained – though the two often coincided, for example in opinions on women's abilities. This combination tended to produce theories that opposed state coercion and old aristocratic elites, and instead argued for the desirability of liberalism, republicanism and democracy, along with toleration in religion. English philosophers were at the forefront of these debates, with John Locke being particularly influential. In his *Letter Concerning Toleration*, published in 1689, Locke argued against Thomas Hobbes' view that uniformity of religion was essential for a peaceful society. On the contrary, Locke believed, toleration would prevent unrest since it would avoid confrontation over religious matters. Even Locke, however, didn't think that religious tolerance should be extended to Catholics or to atheists (though he later modified his views on atheists).

These political and academic debates on tolerance continued for much of the next 200 years, tied in as they were with developing thought about the role of the state, the rights and responsibilities of citizens or subjects, and the developing cultural emphasis on individualism. The increasing intra-religious debates on new scientific advances, such as Darwin's theory of evolution (published in 1859), or new approaches to biblical scholarship, also contributed. Since different religious authorities disagreed with one another on such matters, the idea of a monolithic official faith was increasingly problematic.

Also in 1859, the English philosopher and political theorist John Stuart Mill published *On Liberty*, a treatise on the extent to which the state should interfere with individuals. Mill's work included arguments for the (still controversial) view that religion could never, and should never, be mandated by the state.

In England, the Toleration Act of 1689 had allowed freedom of worship to Nonconformists but clearly excluded Catholics from its terms. The succession crisis of the late seventeenth century (see page 98) had clearly shown that Roman Catholicism was still unacceptable to the country. The folk memory of things like the burnings under Queen Mary (immortalized for future generations in the popular *Foxe's Book of Martyrs*), combined with long-established political distrust of France and Spain, and competing economic and imperial interests, meant that Catholics were indelibly the enemy in the minds of most English people over this period. This began to change slowly after the death of James Stuart in 1766, when the papacy finally recognized the Hanoverian dynasty as the lawful rulers of Britain. As a result, in 1778 the first Catholic Relief Act was passed. This provided that, subject to an oath of loyalty to the crown, Roman Catholics were officially permitted to own property, inherit land, and join the army. Popular reaction against this was fierce in places, with riots in protest taking place in Scotland and London, and Roman Catholics did not finally achieve full political emancipation in England until 1829.

Church, state and atheism

In North America, though some of the early settlers had hoped to establish their own particular type of religion as the only permissible one, it rapidly became clear that in most places such attempts were unsustainable. This was due both to the sheer variety of beliefs and practices held by wave after wave of immigrants (and indeed, the variety of new local church inventions), and the very high mobility of populations. In some of the older established colonies of New England, something like the Church of England remained officially established as the religion of the elite: in Maryland, Virginia and New York, for example, an established church remained part of the new State Constitutions written after the Declaration of Independence from Britain in 1776. But, in practice, after the initial colonial period of the seventeenth century there was rarely any attempt to limit religion. The 1788 US Constitution famously enshrined the principle that no religious test would ever be required as a qualification for state office holders.

In France, the relationship between church and state was tested almost to destruction during the revolutionary period at the end of the eighteenth century. Under the *ancien régime* – the pre-revolutionary system of rule by absolute monarchy in alliance with aristocratic and religious hierarchies – the church had been extremely rich and powerful, owning around 10 per cent of the country's land. The Revolution (1789–99) challenged this whole hierarchical system of rule, and the church was inevitably implicated. In 1789 tithing (church taxation) was abolished and all church property was nationalized; in 1790 religious orders were dissolved and clergy became state employees. Radical attempts were then made, under Robespierre's 'Reign of Terror' (1793–4), to go even further and entirely remove Christianity from the country, a policy known as dechristianization. It was suggested that Christianity might be replaced by a civic Cult of Reason, or a non-specific Cult of the Supreme Being. But these attempts went too far for the majority of the population and, along with the atrocities of the regime (and widespread famine due to attempts to control prices), contributed to Robespierre's fall.

Finally, in 1801, the new dictator-emperor, Napoleon Bonaparte, achieved a Concordat with the Catholic Church which set the pattern for the relationship between church and state in France until the beginning of the twentieth century. In this, most of the state gains of the revolutionary period were cemented: confiscated church property remained the property of the state, and clergy remained state servants. The only concessions were that Catholicism was recognized as the majority religion (though notably not the state religion, so Protestants had equal status as citizens), and Sundays and some feast days were reinstated as public holidays. Bonaparte's imperial ambitions led to Europe-wide war in the first decades of the nineteenth century, and these led to a major shift in the balance of power between the major denominational groupings. In Chadwick's elegant summary:

> Before Napoleon Bonaparte the balance of power in Europe still lay, as always since the Reformation, just with the Catholics – the great powers, Austria, France, and Spain, set against Britain

and the Protestants of Northern Germany. The fall of Napoleon left Spain no longer a great power, France rather weaker, Britain stronger, North German Protestantism much stronger, Russia, a non-Roman Catholic power, much stronger. (Chadwick, 1992)

The example of Robespierre's Cult of Reason demonstrates the extent to which atheism had become intellectually respectable, if not popular, by the end of the eighteenth century, and also the extent to which it was bound up with a rejection of church and aristocratic power. To some extent this was to do with the perceived truth or credibility of religion. Developments in science and biblical scholarship had shown that not all of the Bible could sensibly be understood as literally true. These developments did not in themselves prevent Christian faith, but they did undermine the credibility of the major institutional churches, which clung stubbornly to traditional understandings long after they had been widely discredited. In addition, however, major revolutionary thinkers attacked the Church not primarily on the grounds that religion was untrue, but on the grounds that it was unhelpful or immoral.

For example, Karl Marx famously derided religion as 'the opium of the people': his criticism was that Christianity taught resignation to one's place in life and thus aided the rich by keeping the poor quiescent. Taking a contrasting position against religion were philosophers such as Nietzsche, who used popular understandings of Darwin's new evolutionary theory to argue that religion was morally corrupting because it protected the weak and thus prevented the natural order of things in which the strong would flourish. Similar arguments were used by theorists of white racial supremacy in the last decade of the nineteenth century and in the early twentieth century, and were strongly implicated in the atrocities of Nazi Germany in the years preceding and during the Second World War.

Both atheism and challenges to the role of the Church in public life grew in strength and in geographical breadth over the course of the nineteenth and into the twentieth century. The mid nineteenth century was a period of widespread revolutionary upheaval across Europe, and in these upheavals the Church was most often seen as an enemy to progress. Christianity, and especially the established church, was widely perceived as inseparable from the conservatism and elitism of past hierarchies. For example, in the revolutionary atmospheres of Spain and Italy in the 1840s the churches were widely attacked. In Spain, 38 out of 59 dioceses had no bishop in 1846, while the pope and the Jesuit order both had to flee from Rome in 1848.

Even in places where the role of religion itself was not challenged, similar patterns of state control being exerted over churches were to be seen. In South America, for example, this was a period of struggle for independence in which the nature of the relationship between church and state was called into question, often for the first time since the Spanish authorities had established their firmly Catholic colonies there two or three centuries earlier. In the Orthodox Christian world, the Russian emperor Peter had abolished the Patriarchate of Moscow as early as 1721, and had established a Synod firmly under state control, a situation which survived until the revolution of 1917. Elsewhere in the Orthodox east of Europe a similar pattern of national churches under state patronage and control emerged in many places, such as Greece, out of the nineteenth-century revolutionary ferment.

Industrialization and urbanization

During the Industrial Revolution (roughly dated from 1790 to 1860 in the United Kingdom, where the phenomenon began and was most marked), towns dramatically increased in size as factory working became increasingly common. As a result, patterns of home and social life were changed irreversibly. The movement of people from living by farming on the land to specialization in towns had been a feature of European history from the Middle Ages onwards. But the pace of change increased dramatically in the United Kingdom, and then in other parts of western Europe and North America, in the late eighteenth and nineteenth centuries. Since the nineteenth century, urbanization has become a global phenomenon: it is estimated by the United Nations that around 13 per cent of the world's population lived in towns in 1900, a figure that had increased to 49 per cent by 2005 and is rapidly growing. This change has had an important impact on church life, and hence on the ways in which Christianity and the church have been thought about since, both within and outside the Church.

It is important not to romanticize the pre-industrial past, with its domestic-scale pattern of home production, subsistence farming and manorial/feudal social relationships. It was entirely possible for people to starve to death in years of bad harvests (two particularly stark examples being the Irish Famines of 1740–1 and 1845–52, in each of which around 20 per cent of the population perished). Similarly, it is important not to romanticize the relationship that most people would have had with their local parish church in the pre-modern period. The medieval parish system of a local church and parish priest for each small village meant that most people knew where 'their' church was, and would have celebrated the key events of their and their neighbours' lives in that local church. However, it is unclear to what extent the local church was a feature of everyday life beyond such milestones. Legally in many places everyone was supposed to attend their parish church every Sunday. Many would certainly have done so, but the best evidence we have is from middle- and upper-class families and diarists. Household servants (a sizeable proportion of the population), farm labourers and so on may never have been so regular.

The advent and adoption of large-scale factory production and the urbanization that resulted had a major impact on church life. Widespread migration from the countryside to towns meant the disruption of historic bonds of affection and belonging between local people and churches. As towns and cities grew, churches struggled to keep up with the numbers; but it is also notable that many people simply did not go to new churches when they moved. This suggests strongly that belief and religious practice were closely bound up with tradition and family/social links in this period, as Grace Davie's work on the sociology of religion has suggested for the twentieth century (Davie, 2007). This was also the age of the growth of the Sunday outing. As railway networks developed and bicycles became popular, travel on one's only day off increased in popularity; but even those who stayed locally often preferred a Sunday walk in the park to going to church, as the new urban working class enjoyed what relaxation they could. Limited evidence makes estimating church attendance in the pre-modern period virtually impossible, but it is generally agreed that church attendance increased between 1750 and 1850, and declined thereafter. It seems likely that early urbanization made churchgoing easier as there were no longer geographical constraints to be overcome. After 1850, however, people increasingly chose to do other things with their time.

Urbanization also resulted in a new zeal for Christian social action. Poverty and abuse were endemic in these newly expanding towns, and working conditions were often abysmal. While charity had always been a Christian virtue, it had tended to be exercised on a local basis. The new conditions, alongside a growing awareness of similar or worse abuses worldwide, most notably in the slave trade, meant that a new type of Christian social action arose, aimed at changing unjust structures and using legislation to prevent the worst abuses. The best known example is the campaign by William Wilberforce and others to stop slavery, but this is just one example of a wider movement to take Christianity out of the home and into the public life of the towns and international trade, mirroring what was happening with economic production and social life.

A related development was the rise, in response to the growth of Socialist parties across Europe in the late nineteenth and early twentieth centuries, of a specifically Christian Socialism. In Switzerland, for example, in the early years of the twentieth century, Hermann Kutter and Leonhard Ragaz founded an international League of Religious Socialists. They presented socialism as a fresh revelation of God's will for the world, analogous to the Reformation in the history of Christianity. Such views were widely resisted by the institutional churches.

But this new sense that Christianity implied a call to structural, national and even international social action was unstoppable. It developed over the twentieth century into one of the key ways in which the Christian churches worldwide understand their mission. Just as in mission theory today, however, it was always partnered with a more straightforwardly evangelistic impulse. The overseas missions of the Church interacted in complex ways with colonialism, imperialism and trade (see Chapter 9), but also generated a sense of purpose and excitement within the churches, which contributed to this developing understanding of the international relevance and vocation of Christianity.

Conclusion

By 1900, then, the religious landscape and mindset of Europe and North America had been transformed. Even more significantly, the religious monopoly of the medieval concept of Christendom had been broken. Both practically and ideologically, it was no longer possible in most places for a single state church to claim that it was coterminous with Christianity in that place. The development of toleration and of multiple new denominations meant that there was a new sense of religion, in which individuals would exercise free choice. Toleration had also allowed the rise of philosophical atheism, free from the constraints of potential persecution. This, along with increasing encounters with other faiths both at home and abroad, meant that Christianity itself, not simply one's denomination, was beginning to be conceived as a matter of choice, a theme that strengthened considerably in the twentieth century (see Chapter 10).

European dominance and confidence was already beginning to falter by the end of this period. Religion had advanced and retreated, like a tide, over these two centuries, with the revivals of the eighteenth century filling churches, and then the nineteenth century increasingly seeing them emptying. This, along with academic and church disputes over new scientific and biblical scholarship, left many church members and clergy feeling rather bewildered. Matthew Arnold's poem, 'Dover Beach', written in the mid nineteenth century, expresses this well:

> The Sea of Faith
> Was once, too, at the full, and round earth's shore
> Lay like the folds of a bright girdle furled.
> But now I only hear
> Its melancholy, long, withdrawing roar.

However, though the pace of change was bewildering, Christianity had by no means withdrawn. Indeed, the revival and evangelical enthusiasm of the eighteenth century had transformed the religious landscape of the rest of the world. It had also given Christianity a new emphasis on changing unjust social and economic systems, which was to reinvigorate it in the twentieth century.

Questions to ponder

- What similarities and differences do you see between the revival movements of the eighteenth century, and contemporary Christian renewal movements?
- How do you feel about religious toleration?
- In what ways does this chapter shed light on our current religious context?
- How good a thing was the redefinition of the relationship between churches and states in this period?

9

Globalizing Christianity: *c.* 1500–1900

Introduction

In 1500, Christianity was almost entirely a European religion. The expansion of Islam to the south and east had restricted and diminished once thriving Christian communities there, and missionary efforts had been directed northwards instead. As we have seen in Chapter 5, the medieval orders of friars had been making intrepid journeys beyond the European mainland for at least two centuries, but these made little lasting impact. By 1900, however, Christianity was a truly global religion, with an estimated 500 million adherents worldwide. The astonishing global expansion of Christianity which took place over this period was powered by a heady combination of exploration, trade, colonialism and missionary zeal.

While the history of missions has often been clouded by the apparent contamination of the evangelistic impulse with commercial and military interests, it is important not to overstate the extent to which these overlapped. It was at least sometimes the case that European commercial and military interests found their missionary compatriots to be a confounded nuisance, liable to protect and voice the interests of local people in a way that conflicted with more worldly concerns. From time to time there are examples of missionaries, and even on occasion religious leaders at home, protesting about particularly gross examples of inhuman treatment and abuse. However, such protests were usually both sporadic and largely ineffective in the face of the potential financial and political gains. Alongside these positive voices, of course, much missionary work was seriously compromised by association with military forces imposing European territorial and economic expansion. This had important consequences both for its effectiveness at the time and for its later reputation. The extent to which different missions were tainted by such factors varied a great deal, both by region and across time.

Early exploration and conquest: Spain and Portugal

At the very end of the fifteenth century, rising European wealth and confidence led to a new interest in overseas exploration. Portuguese trading ships were active along the African coast from before 1434, when the first cargo of slaves reached Lisbon. Both Spain and Portugal were determined to find ways to access and tax the lucrative spice trade. Until this point this had been mainly in eastern hands, and was primarily routed to European markets, and thus taxed, through the Italian city states of Genoa and Venice. In 1492, Christopher Columbus sailed west from Spain in search of a westward passage to the East Indies. He landed in the Caribbean, and at first believed that he had reached his intended destination, calling the islands the 'West Indies'. To avoid conflict between the two major Catholic European powers of Spain and Portugal, in the following year the pope proposed a line down the Atlantic, dividing all newly discovered territories in future between the two – Spain in the west, Portugal in the east. This line was altered slightly in 1494, with the Treaty of Tordesillas, but thereafter proved remarkably enduring. Spain was left to conquer the Americas (apart from Brazil, which was east of the line and thus Portuguese), while Portugal concentrated on opening up new trading routes to Africa and India. A further treaty had to be agreed in 1529, establishing a similar line on the other side of the world, after the Spanish succeeded in reaching India from the west, thus proving that the world was a globe, not flat.

For both Spain and Portugal, exporting Christianity was regarded as a given in these adventures. Evangelism was both a justification, and an additional motivation, for the excitement and rewards of exploration. However, it is clear that territorial expansion and financial gain were at least as important. In 1510 the Spanish Council of Castile authorized a document, the 'Requerimiento', to be read to the natives whenever new territories were encountered, heedless of the fact that its Spanish would have been incomprehensible to its hearers. The document begins by describing the Spanish king and queen as 'subduers of the barbarous nations'. It goes on to summarize Christian belief (or at least, the doctrines of creation and ecclesiastical authority that were most useful in this context), and argues that since the pope has God's authority, and has used it to give these lands to the Spanish crown, the locals should submit peacefully. If they do so, they will be graciously welcomed as subjects and will not be compelled to become Christians. But if they refuse, the document concludes, they will be conquered, enslaved, looted – 'and we protest that the deaths and losses which shall accrue from this are your fault' (Restall, 2003). One conquistador who left his own account of these early days, Bernal Diaz del Castillo (1492–1581), described his own motivation as being both 'to give light to those who were in darkness, and to grow rich' (McManners, 1992).

The Spanish conquests in Central and South America were very rapid. By 1515, the whole of the West Indies was under Spanish control, and over the next two decades the Aztec and Inca empires (of modern-day Mexico and Peru) were conquered. Mass conversions, and widespread destruction of old temples and idols, followed. The conquests were often brutal, and attended by many atrocities, and there was widespread abuse of the native population. The Spanish crown increasingly came to rely on the income from the new territories, both from silver mining and from farming, and the practice of forced labour from the locals – stopping only just short of slavery – followed. It is hard to disentangle the work of evangelism from the brutality of the conquest, and to do so fully would be anachronistic. However, it should be noted that much of the evidence that we have for the brutality of the regime comes from the protests of friars working as missionaries in these areas. The most famous of these was Bartolomé de las Casas, a Dominican who devoted much of his life to travelling back and forth between Spain and the West Indies, protesting about the ill-treatment of the native population. His *Short Account of the Destruction of the Indies*, published in 1542, scandalized many with its graphic descriptions of atrocities. As a result new laws were passed to protect the native population, though these were only scantily enforced in the colonies themselves.

The Portuguese encountered a very different context in their territories to the east of the mid-Atlantic line, and lacked the military capacity to emulate the Spanish South American empire. Instead, they established a commercial trading empire, based on a network of fortified port towns along the coast, especially in Goa. The Portuguese were widely hated by the local inhabitants of these areas, partly because of brutal and corrupt behaviour, but primarily because their commercial success was underpinned by the slave trade. This grew throughout the sixteenth and seventeenth centuries, particularly after the Portuguese began to exploit Brazil to grow sugar. Sugar was a labour-intensive crop, and its profitable cultivation was only possible using large numbers of slaves imported from Africa. While Jesuit missionaries (see below) in Brazil tried to protect local converts, and protested throughout the seventeenth century about the ill-treatment of the native population and of slaves, these complaints were largely ignored in the face of the profits being made.

Christianity spread much more slowly in the Portuguese than the Spanish territories. Missionary clergy had little success in the rough frontier cultures of the trading ports, and found their efforts beyond these enclaves undermined by the local inhabitants' experiences of European behaviour. Apart from the example of the Paravas, a society in southern India which in the 1530s converted en masse to Christianity in exchange for Portuguese protection from other aggressors, most places resisted Christianity as being the religion of the oppressors. Furthermore, the religious context in which the Portuguese were operating was not one of primitive paganism, but of the well-established spiritual traditions of the East such as Hinduism and Buddhism. Adherents of these religions were not only able to debate with Christian missionaries on a philosophical and intellectual level, but were also experienced in encountering and absorbing other religions. In addition, as already noted, in some places the Portuguese encountered ancient Christian traditions which had developed independently from western European Christianity.

The Jesuits: missionary experimentation in Japan

The Society of Jesus, better known as the Jesuits, was founded as part of the Roman Catholic response to the Reformation, and dominated mission in the later sixteenth and seventeenth centuries. Francis Xavier (1506–52), one of the first members of the Jesuits, was a remarkably well-travelled missionary himself. He began his career by devising simple liturgies in the local language for the Paravas, and went on to work in both Ceylon and Japan; he died while awaiting permission to enter China.

Xavier's key insight came while in Japan. At first, missionaries to Japan were hopeful that this could be a fertile ground for Christianity. A civilized, literate and spiritual culture greeted them, and they were heard with respect and interest. However, the value in which this ancient culture was held meant that Christianity made little headway when conversion meant rejecting Japanese culture and instead adopting European Christian customs. Instead, Xavier proposed to make Christianity more acceptable to the Japanese by keeping any aspect of local culture that did not directly contradict Christian teaching. He even retained ancestor worship ceremonies, which he deemed to be essentially social rather than religious rituals. Jesuits in Japan therefore adopted the status and dress of Zen priests, and adhered strictly to the dictates of traditional Japanese etiquette. Xavier also had some success in converting individual local nobles by appealing to the relationship between their cult of honour and Christian teachings. By 1600 there were around 300,000 Christians in Japanese churches, particularly around Nagasaki, and three Japanese Christians had been ordained as priests.

By this date, however, Christianity – perhaps partly because of its success – began to be regarded as a threat to the long-term stability of a newly unified Japan. Dutch and English traders were beginning to establish bases there, and Christianity was seen as an element of the expansionist threat that they posed. In 1614 and 1616 a pair of edicts banned Christian worship, and began a period of cruel persecution, in which it is estimated that 62 missionaries and around 2,000 Japanese converts were tortured to death. These persecutions were so effective that by 1639 there was no active Christian presence in Japan, and thereafter all contact between Japan and the outside world was very strictly controlled until the mid nineteenth century. Xavier's culturally adaptive policy was experimented with elsewhere, notably in China, until papal policy changed in the late seventeenth century. The Jesuit ascendancy came to an end when the pope officially denounced the Japanese experiment in 1701. As a direct result of this denunciation, missionaries to China were abruptly expelled. The Jesuit order was formally abolished by the papacy in 1773.

Protestant corporate colonialism

The great Catholic powers of Spain and Portugal dominated world trade and mission in the sixteenth century, but in the seventeenth century their dominance was challenged by England and the Dutch Republic. England began in the 1580s by attempting to found colonies in North America; although these initial attempts, at Roanoke, failed, others from the 1590s onwards were successful. Statements at the time about the benefits of colonialism listed Protestant missions to counteract the Spanish Catholic influence alongside more pragmatic concerns such as increasing English trade, establishing a reliable source of timber and other naval supplies, employing the idle poor and providing a base from which to search for a north-west passage to the spice islands. Descriptions of the new world, aimed at recruiting colonists and investors, emphasized that the local populations were ripe for conversion. Religious mission was seen as an aspect of foreign policy and national self-interest; as well as genuine missionary zeal there was considerable competitive desire to break the Catholic (particularly the Spanish) monopoly on trade, faith and gold.

However, for both England and the Dutch Republic, colonialism was essentially a commercial activity. Shares were issued in companies which were then granted licences and monopolies by the government to exploit certain territories overseas. This commercial principle had been established from the beginning, even before the major East India Companies were created. There was never the same degree of crown control of these enterprises as was the case with Spain and Portugal, largely because the crown did not have the funds available to pay for the ventures and so there was a need to attract investors. For example, Sir Walter Raleigh negotiated a contract between himself, the crown and his principal investors in 1584, specifying how profits would be divided.

The English East India Company, founded in 1600, was the first of the new breed of major joint stock enterprise companies which were the vehicle for European dominance of world trade and colonialism over the coming centuries. It was swiftly followed by many others, such as the Dutch East India Company in 1602, the Virginia Company in 1606, and the Dutch West India Company in 1621. Such corporations were granted quasi-governmental powers in the vast areas that they came to dominate, being permitted by their founding charters to raise armies, build fortifications, and wage war as necessary for their defence.

Christianity spread with these overseas activities in three main ways. Some colonial initiatives were accompanied by official government-sponsored clergy, there to establish churches in the new colonies and to spread the gospel to the native populations that would be encountered. Others had private clergy appointed by the merchant adventurers responsible with a similar remit. Not all ships were accompanied by such clergy, but in their absence it was usually the case that the ship's captain or officers would lead services on the voyage and in the colonies. In this way the Church of England and the Dutch Reformed tradition were rapidly exported worldwide. The earliest known Anglican church outside the British Isles, St Peter's Church in Bermuda, was established in 1612, and there are many early records of the Book of Common Prayer being used on board ship and in the first English colonies. Experiences in the colonies also fed back, to a limited extent, into the religious life in the old world. For example, when the Book of Common Prayer was revised in 1662 the new preface noted that some changes had been made to meet the needs of the new colonies, mainly in the provision of a service of baptism for those 'of riper years', useful for baptizing 'natives on our plantations and other converts to the faith'.

The religious differences and rivalries of the old world were often also exported to the new colonies, although sometimes attempts were made deliberately to promote a greater tolerance in these frontier and missionary contexts. For example, England's first truly successful proprietary colony (privately owned under licence from the crown) was Maryland, founded by George Calvert in 1632. Calvert had recently converted to Roman Catholicism, and tried to create a colony in which both Catholics and Protestants could flourish together. The first group of colonists included both denominations, and Calvert's letters of instruction emphasized the need to avoid religious disputes, as well as giving the settlers directions about defence, planting and the development of a mixed economy. Maryland was unable to avoid religious conflict entirely, however: the Jesuits were extremely unhappy with Calvert's policy of tolerance and began to buy areas of land and declare them to be Catholic. In 1641, Calvert took sweeping measures against the Jesuit agitators, confiscating all their land beyond that needed for their subsistence and insisting that they accept his authority. Astonishingly, he won papal support for these policies. At the same time, Puritan refugees from England began to settle in Maryland, and quickly came to dominate the local legislature. The conflict of the English Civil War was mirrored in Maryland, and in 1648 Calvert was forced to agree to a compromise: from now on, half the Governor's Council would be Protestant.

One of the major theological questions that the colonies raised in the seventeenth century was slavery. Slavery was not widespread in the North American colonies until the mid seventeenth century, but thereafter changing economic circumstances rapidly led to its widespread adoption. Initially, this was justified on religious grounds. The terminology of the first half of the century classified people as 'Christians' or others. Black Christians were initially seen primarily as Christians in this classification; there were several instances of free black Christians, such as Anthony Johnson, becoming prosperous landowners in their own right in the early seventeenth century. As slavery became increasingly widespread, however, after 1660 there was fierce debate about how converted slaves should be treated.

The evangelistic impulse had a perverse impact on this debate. Some missionaries and theologians argued for slavery to be justified on the grounds of race, because they were concerned that they might be barred from evangelizing among slaves if owners couldn't afford for them to convert. As a result, by the end of the seventeenth century slavery was mainly justified on racial grounds, and conversion was seen as irrelevant to a slave's economic and social status.

This was an uncomfortable conclusion for many. In particular, it was in conflict with the view that all Christians – if not all human beings – were 'brothers'. This view was increasingly common in the new denominations such as Methodism and Quakerism that began to develop at the end of the seventeenth and over the eighteenth century, which partly defined themselves against the established churches by their lack of hierarchy. These new denominations played an important role in the growing abolition movements.

The missionary societies

The eighteenth and nineteenth centuries, as noted in the previous chapter, were a great age of religious revival. One notable aspect of this revival was the foundation of many missionary societies, often primarily supported by the laity, which sought to evangelize the vast colonies and the rest of the world. Two of the earliest societies, still active today, were the Society for Promoting Christian Knowledge (SPCK), founded in 1698, and the Society for the Propagation of the Gospel (SPG) in 1701. These early societies were sometimes notable for their ecumenical co-operation. In 1709, for example, SPCK sent a printer and printing press to India to help produce the Tamil translation of the Bible created by German Lutheran missionaries. The later British and Foreign Bible Society, founded in 1804 to produce foreign-language Bibles (initially for the Welsh, but soon for India and worldwide), was also committed to ecumenical working from the beginning. Others, however, soon found themselves in competition with missionaries from different denominations. For example, SPG, which was founded to send priests and teachers to the North American colonies, soon found itself in direct competition with the new denominations of the Great Revival.

The work of these missionary societies differed markedly from earlier missionary techniques. These were voluntary and unofficial societies, and so had no authority to impose Christianity by force. Furthermore, by this period the existence of different denominations and even different faiths was largely recognized as a given, in the Enlightenment atmosphere of (relative) toleration and individualism. Missionaries of all denominations therefore used the methodology of the evangelical revival movement, aiming at individual conversion and the building up of a committed core of disciples, however small. The provision of charitable services such as schools and hospitals was also very common, replicating the traditional services that churches provided in Europe.

These missionary endeavours were often dramatically successful. Despite all the handicaps of being associated with external colonial powers, and often requiring the rejection of cultural norms and practices, Christianity was widely embraced by those who heard it. And by 1900, the dedication of the missionary societies to making sure that everyone had heard it had paid off. By that date there was virtually no part of Africa, for example, where Christianity had not been preached and won converts, and by the mid twentieth century it is estimated that somewhere between a third and a half of the population of most countries of Sub-Saharan Africa were Christians.

The export of Christianity was clearly welcomed by many, and was by no means the worst aspect of colonialism and European imperialism. Indeed, many missionaries were motivated by an opposition to these, and tried to mitigate their worst effects. The Methodist missionary Thomas Jenkins provides a good example both of this, and of the ambivalence that such missionaries faced. Jenkins became a trusted adviser to the Mpondo ruler, to the east of Cape Colony, and for many years helped to maintain peace on the frontier and, by opposing colonial expansion, the independence of the Mpondo people. Nevertheless, when it became clear that the colony was determined to expand, he stood aside, feeling that his loyalties wouldn't allow him to actively oppose European dominance.

Jenkins' example also demonstrates the extent to which missionaries were often much further ahead than government or trade representatives in understanding local cultures, languages and politics. Another English missionary, John Philip of the London Missionary Society, who struggled to assert the rights of Southern Africans in the 1820s and 1830s, was repeatedly found to be more accurate in his assessment of local situations and issues than the official reports.

Nevertheless, it is clear that many missionaries, alongside their government and commercial European colleagues, were remarkably ignorant of local conditions and – with hindsight – breathtakingly arrogant about the benefits of European culture, which was too often considered to be inseparable from the benefits of Christianity. Christianity appears to have been considered as one beneficial and demonstrably superior European export among many – one which, like British engineering, would infallibly be seen to be superior to whatever the local culture could manufacture. Some of this was literally unthinking, the result of a collective cultural blindspot that simply took the forms of religion that Europe was used to for granted. For example, even Henry Venn (the Secretary of the Church Mission Society from 1841 to 1872), who was remarkably forward-thinking in his missionary theory and aimed to create in every area 'a self-supporting, self-governing, self-propagating native church', seems simply to have assumed that such churches would use the Book of Common Prayer (Ward, 2006).

The Anglican Communion

The British Empire expanded across much of the globe in the late eighteenth and nineteenth centuries, superseding the earlier dominance of Spain, Portugal and the Dutch Republic. The work of the missionary societies ensured that the Christianity of the Church of England spread worldwide with it. At first, all colonial churches were under the jurisdiction of the Bishop of London, but this rapidly became unsustainable and colonial bishops began to be appointed in the late eighteenth century. The first Church of England bishop outside of England was the Bishop of Nova Scotia, appointed in 1787. In 1814, there was an Anglican Bishop of Calcutta; in 1824, a Bishop of the West Indies; and in 1836, a Bishop of Australia. The pace of establishment of colonial dioceses quickly increased, and in 1841 a Colonial Bishoprics Council was established.

In some colonies initially the Church of England was the established church, but this was never universal. In 1861 it was ruled that (except where it was specifically established) the Church of England had the same legal position as all other denominations in the colonies. Thereafter, Anglican churches abroad were in a very different position from that of the Church of England, and evolved differently and independently. Generally speaking both the mission agencies and the Church of England bishops believed that local leadership was a good thing and was to be encouraged as soon as possible, and in time local bishops began to be appointed. As dioceses spread they became naturally grouped into provinces, under archbishops, and national synods began to legislate independently. The examples of America, Canada and Nigeria illustrate the very different histories of some of this family of churches.

In America, after the War of Independence (1775–83) the church naturally had to become independent of crown control. The Episcopal Church was therefore established to replace the Church of England, headed by the British monarch, with an alternative ecclesiastical structure. The first Anglican bishop in North America was Samuel Seabury, who secured his consecration from the Scottish Episcopal Church in 1784. Anglicanism was never, except in a few areas of New England, the established church; and even where it was the official religion, it was in practice only the religion of the elite. The proliferation of denominations in the Great Awakening meant that the American religious landscape was from very early on characterized by variety, diversity and choice.

After the War of Independence many of the defeated loyalists fled to Canada, and Anglicans were numerous among these. As a result, the Church of England became synonymous with the church in Canada, despite the fact that Canada was not strictly speaking British territory. The first Church of England bishop outside England was one of these refugees, Charles Inglis, who was consecrated as Bishop of Nova Scotia in 1787. The anomalous position of the Church of

England in Canada caused considerable unrest from members of other denominations, particularly over land privileges given to Anglican clergy. As a result, the church in Canada was disestablished in the 1850s, giving all denominations equal civil rights. Until 1955, however, the Anglican Church of Canada was officially titled 'The Church of England in the Dominion of Canada'.

In Nigeria, the first Church of England mission arrived in 1842, and a local church was quickly established. Henry Venn, Secretary of the Church Mission Society, was convinced of the value of indigenous leadership, and championed the ministry of Samuel Crowther, a Yoruba freed slave who was already studying for ordination in London at the time. In 1864 he was consecrated Bishop of the Niger. Crowther's ministry was by all accounts a great success, but problems began when a different group of missionaries arrived in 1887 and began to evangelize in competition with the existing diocesan structures. These new missionaries were convinced that Crowther's patient and gentle missionary work and dialogue with Islam were a disgrace, and after his death they campaigned hard (and successfully) for him not to be replaced by another African. When a European bishop was appointed, some Yoruba Christians were so incensed by CMS's backtracking on its earlier commitment to local leadership that they formed independent churches; only in the 1950s was another African bishop appointed. Perhaps as a result of this infighting and loss of nerve, the church grew only slowly: in 1900, it is estimated that there were around 35,000 Christians in Nigeria, perhaps 0.2 per cent of the population. In the last decades of the twentieth century, however, the church in Nigeria became the fastest growing church in the Anglican Communion, accounting for around 18 per cent of the population in 2000.

As new dioceses and provinces began to be established, and to develop increasingly independently from the middle of the nineteenth century, the question of what held the churches together began to be asked. The only parameters of Anglican identity were the use of the Book of Common Prayer and the 39 Articles, while the Archbishop of Canterbury was looked to for leadership effectively by default. The first Lambeth Conference was held, in 1867, in the context of a widespread desire to condemn Bishop Colenso of Natal for his unorthodoxy.

Colenso had been appointed bishop of the new diocese of Natal in 1852, a diocese that had been financed by fundraising by Bishop Gray, the first Bishop of Cape Town, and SPG. Bishop Gray was therefore horrified to discover that he had appointed someone he came to view as a heretic. Colenso threw himself into mission to the Zulu people, and was innovative in working to inculturate Christianity. He was assisted by a number of native speakers, especially William Ngidi, and was criticized for allowing Ngidi's questions to shape his thinking. But most controversial was his commentary on Romans, which went beyond the bounds of accepted orthodoxy on sin and justification. In 1863 the Church in South Africa declared him a heretic, but Colenso appealed to the British courts, arguing that his was a crown appointment not Bishop Gray's. He won his case and remained in post, to the chagrin of Bishop Gray.

The case of Colenso raised questions not only of orthodoxy, but of provincial autonomy. The Church of Canada, which had taken a lead in condemning Colenso, led calls for a meeting which would give definitive leadership. However, some bishops were reluctant to attend, fearing that it would become a legislative body and compromise their local autonomy. A commitment was made by the Archbishop of Canterbury, therefore, that the conference would be only consultative, and that any resolutions would be simply advisory.

The Lambeth Conference met again in 1888, and at that meeting made its most enduring statement, the Lambeth Quadrilateral. This set out the four bases of Anglican identity (the Bible, the creeds, the two sacraments of baptism and communion, and the historic episcopate), and was originally intended to provide a basis for discussions with the Roman Catholic and Orthodox Churches. Incidentally, it established the most widely accepted parameters of Anglican identity.

Conclusion

Over these 400 years, Christianity spread around the world in a bewildering variety of ways. It was thrust upon whole peoples at the point of a sword; adopted as a form of protection; taught to natives as if to children; explained to sages of other faiths; commended through charitable (and sometimes paternalistic) works; and translated into languages around the world, some of which had first to have a written form devised. Difficult questions about to what extent local customs could be disentangled from beliefs were faced, and different answers were experimented with. Repeatedly, well-intentioned missionaries in a variety of contexts found that profit and power tended to triumph over piety; but repeatedly, too, missionaries were prepared to protest about the worst abuses, and perhaps mitigate the worst effects. Despite the mixed motivations and often tragic stories that accompanied much of the European expansion of these centuries, Christianity was preached worldwide, and was in many places welcomed and adopted wholeheartedly. Both the successes and the failings of the missionary enterprises of these centuries set the context for the story of Christianity in the twentieth and twenty-first centuries.

Questions to ponder

- What aspects of the growth and spread of Christianity in this period might we be able to learn from today – both positively and negatively?
- What were the strengths and weaknesses of the Jesuits' Japanese experiment?
- How do you feel about the history of European missions?
- In what ways does this chapter shed light on our current religious context?

10

Conclusion: Christianity after *c.* 1900

Introduction

In the twentieth and twenty-first centuries Christianity has changed, and changed its own self-understanding, at an often bewildering pace. In the first place, it has grown remarkably: from around 500 million adherents in 1900 to around 2 billion in 2000, nearly a third of the world's population. This growth has shifted the centre of gravity away from western Europe, where Christianity had been concentrated since the Middle Ages. It is often said that the typical Anglican is now a young African woman, and a similar shift in geographical weight has also taken place in both Catholicism and newer denominations such as Pentecostalism. Christianity has also grown rapidly in China and neighbouring states such as Korea, since the second half of the twentieth century. Such growth has confounded the belief, increasingly frequently expressed over the course of the twentieth century until its final decade, that secularism was rapidly spreading and that Christianity, and indeed religion in general, was an outdated mindset that would soon be eclipsed or eradicated.

Apart from this growth, several other major trends can be identified. The development of the ecumenical movement, encouraging different denominations to work more closely together, was a major achievement of the twentieth century. The two world wars of the first half of the century are still having an impact on Christianity around the world. This is most obvious in the social changes that they began or accelerated, notably in gender relations but also in demographics and social order. The world wars also influenced the major theological trends of the twentieth century, which include a re-evaluation of Jewish–Christian relations and a new emphasis on the doctrines of the incarnation and the Trinity. Christians in many places around the world are still experiencing the impact of the ending of colonialism. Finally, the fragmentation of cultures and, conversely, the increasing globalization of culture or at least of communications and economics, in the later twentieth century, has led both to a new emphasis on international economic justice, and to increasing tensions between different cultural expressions of Christianity.

Ecumenism

The ecumenical movement is one of the greatest achievements of twentieth-century Christianity, even though it has not yet fulfilled the hopes of its early proponents for formal unity between different denominations. Nevertheless, it has had some limited successes in formal unity (notably the united churches in South India and Bangladesh). More broadly, it has borne fruit in the active co-operation and lack of antagonism between denominations locally that would have been inconceivable at the beginning of the century.

The origins of the ecumenical movement lie in the trends discussed in Chapter 8. The development of the idea of toleration, the proliferation of denominations, the decoupling of Christianity from national identity, and the revival and pietist movements which cut across denominational boundaries, can all be seen to have contributed. These factors resulted in a partial reversal of the confessionalization of Europe of the Reformation period, as countries could no longer convincingly identify themselves as monolithically Protestant or Catholic. Increasingly, Christians identified as Christians first, with a partial weakening in some areas of denominational allegiances. Even where this was not the case, there was in most places an increased desire to work together across denominational boundaries, for the sake of more effective mission both at home and abroad. Ecumenical questions were first raised formally as a result of the missionary experience in India in the nineteenth century. Here, Christianity's lack of progress in what had seemed at first to be receptive territory was ascribed to the very visible differences and competition between missionaries of different denominations.

An organized ecumenical movement began in 1910, when representatives of several churches gathered for a Missionary Conference in Edinburgh. The excitement and impetus generated from this conference led to a variety of other initiatives in ecumenical discussion. For example, in Anglicanism the 1920 Lambeth Conference pronounced that ecumenism should be encouraged, and this bore particular fruit in the establishment of the Church of South India. This was the first ever union of episcopal and non-episcopal churches, that is, churches organized around and led by bishops and those that had rejected bishops at the Reformation. Anglican, Methodist, Congregational, Presbyterian and Reformed churches all united in a common mission to the nation, when India received formal independence from the British Empire in 1947.

Similar currents of thought culminated in the foundation of the World Council of Churches in 1948, and indirectly contributed to other initiatives such as the Universal Declaration of Human Rights. While the world's largest denomination, the Roman Catholic Church, continues to be uncertain about how to classify other denominations – being notably reluctant to use the word 'churches' – and is not a full member of the World Council of Churches, it participates in all its discussions as an observer.

The general lowering of the temperature in Catholic–Protestant dialogue worldwide is a major achievement of the ecumenical movement. At the beginning of the twentieth century anti-Catholic feeling was still running high in some areas, notably and destructively in parts of Northern Ireland (where in some areas it still lingers). Despite the disappointment felt by some lifelong enthusiasts for ecumenism at the lack of formal unity, the grass-roots co-operation that is often now the case between denominations is remarkable. Other collaborations have also been successful: the united Church of South India has been joined by other united churches such as that of Bangladesh; the Lutheran churches have joined in a World Federation, and have formed various ecumenical links, notably with Anglicanism in the Porvoo Agreement.

Furthermore, and perhaps more importantly, major campaigning movements such as the Jubilee 2000 campaign for debt-relief in the Global South, and the fair trade movement, have been successful in gaining co-ordinated support and backing from all the major denominations. Interest seems to have shifted in recent years, from official discussions and plans for formal unity (which too often have foundered on what seem to most lay people to be relatively obscure technical points over church organization or points of doctrine), to what the various churches can do together. The technical term for this new focus is orthopraxis (correct actions), rather than orthodoxy (correct beliefs). The ability and willingness of the churches to get together to act and speak in global politics and aid at the turn of the twenty-first century must be largely credited to the groundwork put in over the twentieth century by committed ecumenists.

The world wars' legacy: social upheaval

It would be hard to over-estimate the impact of the two world wars. For the history of Christianity, they have had several major results. The ecumenical movement just discussed was of course given additional impetus by the general view that such destruction must not be allowed to happen again, spurring new efforts for international co-operation. But two other effects of the wars have also been particularly dominant in church affairs since the second half of the twentieth century: social changes and theological changes.

The social upheaval caused by the two wars is well known. The loss of life in the First World War (coupled with the influenza epidemic that followed) caused immense demographic shifts in the countries affected, with a high proportion of young men being killed. The gender imbalance that this caused, when compounded with the Second World War and the subsequent need for women to be engaged in war work, contributed to a dramatic acceleration in the shifting expectations of gender roles in Europe.

In addition, the heavy taxation needed to fund the war effort, and new military technology and experiences which were shared by aristocracy and commoners side by side, both contributed to a huge social shift. The culture and economy of domestic service, which had dominated life in previous centuries, vanished. Hand in hand with this went a new irreverence for authority. This change in attitude was born in the industrial age of the previous century with its new bourgeoisie, but came to maturity in the first half of the twentieth century. The horrors of war caused both a new sense of entitlement in those who contributed to or suffered in the war effort, and a new appreciation of the equal value of all human lives (seen for example in the Declaration of Human Rights).

Both of these social changes also contributed, with medical advances which reduced infant and maternal mortality, and effective contraception, to a striking change in expectations of family life. Over the twentieth century there developed a new emphasis on a relatively small 'nuclear family', defined by a cosy private home life, and increasingly also by the exercising of free choice in leisure activities and the purchase of consumer goods.

These social changes have been the main driver of the history of Christianity in Europe, and to some extent elsewhere, in the twentieth and twenty-first centuries. Although initial reactions to the horrors of war included a nostalgia which resulted in an increase in church attendance in the 1950s, this was short lived. Church attendance has been under pressure ever since from a combination of social factors. These include a new cult of the 'ideal home', again a development with Victorian middle-class roots which burgeoned in the post-war period. The growth of new suburbs in pursuit of such homes has led to a commuting culture which has pervaded well beyond the middle classes and has contributed to a further decline in traditional parish links. The trend noted in the nineteenth century towards weekends being dedicated to leisure activities rather than church attendance has also continued.

Women going out of the home to work has frequently been cited as a factor in church decline, but it is rarely noted that an even more important cultural change has been among those women who remain at home with children. The changing view of the family has meant that, since the second half of the twentieth century, women at home with small children have increasingly devoted their time to child-centred rather than community-centred activities.

More generally, of course, church attendance and attitudes to Christianity have been deeply affected by the rapid growth of a consumer leisure culture and an individualistic mindset that prioritizes personal choice and pleasure over duty and community (the latter being seen as outdated, unfashionable and even negative concepts). When this shift in attitudes is added to the growth in global travel and growing consciousness of other faiths and cultures through both tourism and immigration, it is easy to see why Christianity has become increasingly conceptualized as a lifestyle choice rather than a foundational truth in twenty-first-century Europe.

The main controversies in the worldwide Christian churches in recent decades have been over the extent to which new understandings of and attitudes to gender and sexuality are compatible with, or should challenge, traditional Christian teaching in these areas. These new attitudes and understandings are inherently linked with the wider changes that have taken place in society since the wars, both in social and medical terms, and also in the extent to which individual/consumer choice has become a major theme of the contemporary 'Western' worldview (and has rapidly been exported worldwide).

An early example of these controversies was the issue of contraception, which was officially forbidden by the Church of England at the beginning of the twentieth century, and is still officially forbidden by the Roman Catholic Church. Controversies over the role of women have played out in various ways in different denominations, notably in recent decades in debates over women's ordination. The flashpoint for anxieties over new gender roles and understandings of family in the Islamic world has mainly been the role of women, but in the Christian churches such anxieties have been most bitterly expressed over homosexuality.

Post-colonialism and political upheaval

The end of the colonial era, in which the British Empire and other European powers politically dominated much of the rest of the world, has had wide-reaching implications. Worldwide, the impact of the withdrawal of colonial powers in an often unplanned, unsystematic and abrupt way, with little attention paid to the geographical boundaries or internal systems left behind, has led to considerable political disruption and often outright war across large swathes of the old empires, especially in parts of Africa such as the Congo. This has led to incalculable human misery and mass displacements of refugees, which has also of course had a considerable impact on churches throughout the continent.

Large numbers of international and inter-continental migrants and refugees have changed the social, cultural and religious contexts in which churches (and indeed other religions) operate. In Britain, for example, not only has the indigenous population grown in awareness of other faiths, but also large numbers of Christians from other cultural backgrounds have become part of the local church context. One of the great lost opportunities of mid twentieth-century European Christianity was the failure of local European churches to adapt to and accommodate a sudden influx of Christian immigrants, who instead tended to react to the lukewarm or even hostile welcome they received by setting up their own style of churches. Most church growth in Britain particularly in the last few decades has been among these new black-led churches.

In the first decades of the twenty-first century, the debate over whether homosexuality is compatible with Christianity, and specifically with ordination, is the presenting issue in threatened schism between various parts of the Anglican Communion, as well as the chosen battleground for debates between liberal and conservative branches of many Christian denominations. From a historical perspective, these divisions appear to be a further outworking of the end of the colonial era and the sudden dismantling of European colonies, particularly of the old British Empire, in the mid twentieth century. It is notable that one of the main charges levelled against liberal voices is that they are attempting a neo-colonial cultural imperialism, and a considerable amount of discomfort at this possibility is felt in European churches. Interestingly, American churches are influential on both sides of the arguments, and some African churches (notably that of South Africa) are more liberal than others, suggesting that post-colonial interactions are considerably more complex than a first glance might suggest.

The end of the Second World War led to some similar effects within Europe and around the Mediterranean rim. The state of Cold War relations between the United States and the communist powers of Russia and parts of Europe led to considerable tensions throughout the continent. The Balkan states in particular were left in a fragile and unstable situation throughout much of the twentieth century, which sporadically erupted in massacres and even systematic 'ethnic cleansing'. The establishment of the State of Israel, after the horrors of the anti-semitic Holocaust in Nazi Germany became clear, was greeted with wide acclaim, but has again led to considerable tension and much human misery in the region. The ancient Christian churches of Palestine are only just clinging on to existence.

Theological trends

The two world wars also had a major impact on Christian theology over the following decades. On the one hand, there was a widespread revulsion against the possibility of the existence of a good God and certainly of the sort of 'national mascot' God that had frequently been invoked. This disquiet was first expressed as a result of the huge numbers who died in the First World War, and then intensified after the Second World War, when the horrific cruelty and scale of the slaughter of the Holocaust became known. The most pressing question in theology in the immediate post-war period was whether, or how, theology was possible in the face of the Holocaust. How was it possible to conceive of a good God who apparently ignored the prayers of those who were suffering, and who could allow a whole ethnic group (especially the Jews, a group who claimed to have a special relationship with him) to be virtually wiped out? What could usefully be said of such a God, or into such a situation? Out of this introspection and self-examination have come some remarkable new themes in Christian theology.

To some, the only answer to such questions was atheism, as they felt that the very idea of a god had been discredited. To some, it led to a retreat into what has come to be called 'fundamentalism', or extreme conservatism – a reaction against the modern concept of 'progress' which had been seen to have failed. Such views were particularly fostered during the Cold War, with its imminent fears of nuclear holocaust. For others, old habits in theology had to be urgently rethought. For example, national triumphalism in religion needed to be subjected to very close examination, as did the theology and practice of intercessory prayer. The stories of genocide in the Old Testament needed to be re-examined, and the ways in which Christian theology and history had demonized the Jewish people needed to be repented of and corrected.

Subsequent Christian theology has radically changed much of the traditional negative view of Judaism. From the mid to late twentieth century there was a resurgence of interest in the concept of 'Jesus the Jew', and in the first-century Jewish context in which Christian thought and life had developed. Alongside this, in tandem with developing interest in and contact with members of other faiths through immigration and tourism, the relatively new discipline of inter-faith studies is beginning to emerge. Already many university theology faculties have been rebranded as existing for the study of 'theology and religion' or 'religious studies', and the new discipline has already begun to attract conservative critics insisting on the uniqueness of Christianity.

There has also been a very strong trend in post-war theology to emphasize the incarnation and suffering of God in Jesus, rather than the triumph of the resurrection and God's all-powerful heavenly sovereignty. This has been the main answer given to the question of how theology is possible in the light of the Holocaust. It is exemplified most famously by Dietrich Bonhoeffer, whose *Letters and Papers from Prison*, written shortly before his death, literally spoke out of this context.

Another major development has been the emergence of 'liberation theology' in South America, in parallel with the development of self-consciously feminist theologies in North America and Europe, and black theologies in Africa and elsewhere. These have all raised the question of whether and how traditional theologies might have been designed or subverted – either deliberately or unconsciously – to support the agenda of the ruling classes.

When combined with the social trends already discussed towards less rigidly defined gender and family roles, increased immigration and travel, and a less hierarchical understanding of society, which have produced a new theological interest in diversity, these developments have led to a resurgence of interest in the doctrine of the Trinity. The Trinity was largely ignored over the eighteenth and nineteenth centuries, during which the emphasis on scientific enquiry and rationalism meant that its claim to unexaminable mystery was widely seen as an embarrassment. However, since the 1950s the Trinity has increasingly been at the heart of new theological thinking, reconceived as enshrining a principle of diversity and equality at the heart of the Christian understanding of God.

Conclusion

In the late twentieth century, and the first decades of the twenty-first, political and commercial globalism have emerged as major trends to which the churches have not yet worked out an adequate response. Over the course of the twentieth century, the two world wars and the ensuing Cold War led to a new awareness of the extent to which national interests and security were increasingly interdependent. The second half of the twentieth century also saw the rise of international corporations answerable to no single government, and sometimes involved in commercial or monetary activity on a scale larger than many nations. Additionally, the balance of commercial and political power worldwide is shifting rapidly, and the major populations and cultures of the East – which for many centuries quarantined themselves from the rest of the world – look likely to assume a new dominance.

Combined with the rapidly increasing global speed of communications, these developments have led to a new focus in Christianity on issues of worldwide significance, from poverty, oppression and issues of human rights to questions (from the end of the twentieth century) of trade justice and global environmental issues. The history of these contemporary questions cannot yet be written. But just as political and economic trends have shaped the environment in which Christianity has developed, and influenced the many forms it has taken, over the past two thousand years, so it seems certain that the trends outlined here will shape the Church in the decades to come.

Questions to ponder

- What do you think are the most important trends identified in this chapter?
- How important do you think social, economic and political factors are in shaping Christianity?
- How do you feel about the theological developments of the twentieth century?
- What current developments do you think might prove most influential in shaping the future history of Christianity?

References and suggestions
for further reading

Arnold, M. (1994), *Selected Poems*, Penguin, London.

Bonhoeffer, D., Bethge, E., ed., Fuller, R. H., trans. (1956), *Letters and Papers from Prison*, SCM Press, London.

Brown, P. (2003), *The Rise of Western Christendom: Triumph and Diversity, AD 200–1000*, 2nd edn, Blackwell, Oxford,.

Chadwick, O., 'Great Britain and Europe', in McManners, J., ed. (1992), *The Oxford Illustrated History of Christianity*, Oxford University Press, Oxford.

Craigie J., ed. (1982), *Minor Prose Works of King James VI and I*, The Scottish Text Society, Edinburgh.

Davie, G. (2007), *The Sociology of Religion*, Sage, London.

De la Bedoyere, G., ed. (2004), *The Diary of John Evelyn*, Boydell Press, Woodbridge.

Duffy, E. (2005), *The Stripping of the Altars: Traditional Religion in England 1400–1580*, Yale University Press, New Haven and London.

Esler, P., ed. (2000), *The Early Christian World*, 2 vols, Routledge, London.

Green, M. (2004), *Evangelism in the Early Church*, revised edn, William B. Eerdmans, Grand Rapids.

Haigh, C. (1993), *English Reformations: Religion, Politics and Society under the Tudors*, Clarendon Press, Oxford.

Hylson-Smith, K. (1996–8), *The Churches in England from Elizabeth I to Elizabeth II*, 3 vols, SCM, London.

Hylson-Smith, K. (1999–2001), *Christianity in England from Roman times to the Reformation*, 3 vols, SCM, London.

King, J. N., ed. (2009), *Foxe's Book of Martyrs: Select Narratives*, Oxford University Press, Oxford.

Lawler, T. M. C., ed. (1981), *The Complete Works of St. Thomas More*, vol. 6, Yale University Press, New Haven.

Luther, M., 95 Theses, are available in a variety of editions and can be found online in English translation at <www.iclnet.org/pub/resources/text/wittenberg/luther/web/ninetyfive.html>

MacCulloch, D. (2010), *A History of Christianity*, Penguin, London.

McManners, J. (1992), *The Oxford Illustrated History of Christianity*, Oxford University Press, Oxford.

McNeill, J. T., ed. (1960), *Calvin: The Institutes of Christian Religion*, SCM Press, London.

Marshall, P. (2010), *The Reformation: A Very Short Introduction*, Oxford University Press, Oxford.

Neill, S. (1986), *A History of Christian Missions* (Penguin History of the Church), 2nd edn, Penguin, London.

Restall, M. (2003), *Seven Myths of the Spanish Conquest*, Oxford University Press USA, New York.

Rummel, E., ed. (1990), *The Erasmus Reader*, University of Toronto Press, Toronto.

Shirley-Price, L., trans. and ed. (1990), *Bede: Ecclesiastical History of the English People*, Penguin, London.

Stevenson, J., ed. (1966), *Creeds, Councils and Controversies: Documents Illustrative of the History of the Church AD 337–461*, SPCK, London.

Stevenson, J. and Frend, W. H. C., eds (1987), *A New Eusebius: Documents Illustrating the History of the Church to AD 337*, SPCK, London.

Thomas, K. (1978), *Religion and the Decline of Magic*, Penguin, London.

Tyerman, C. (2005), *The Crusades: A Very Short Introduction*, Oxford University Press, Oxford.

Ward, K. (2006), *A History of Global Anglicanism*, Cambridge University Press, Cambridge.

Index

ND - #0054 - 270325 - C0 - 216/138/11 - PB - 9780281066421 - Matt Lamination